Leadership Questions Confronting the Church

BY

JACK P. LEWIS

Christian Communications
P.O. Box 150
Nashville, TN 37202

Christian Communications is a division of the
Gospel Advocate Co., P.O. Box 150, Nashville, TN 37202

ISBN 0-89225-275-8

Table of Contents

Foreword

1. Women Keep Silent in the Church 1
2. Usurp Authority? 7
3. The Authority of Elders 9
4. Greek Words for Elders 13
5. Elders—Lords Over God's Heritage? 37
6. A Self-Perpetuating Board? 43
7. Greek Word Studies on the Function and
    Authority of Preachers 49
8. Preaching As One Having Authority 71
9. The Majority of the Men? 75
10. Tradition 81
11. Reflections on Preaching 87
12. That Which Every Joint Supplies 93
13. When God Says, "You Are Unworthy!" 97
14. The Ministry of Study 101
15. Tell Us the Dream 107

Foreword

These essays on leadership questions confronting the church which are here collected have in some cases been presented previously in lectureships and have earlier appeared in print over several years in various periodicals and books. The reception they received, both from those who criticized and those who applauded, suggested that they would be of use to a wider audience. Gratitude is here expressed to Christian Communications, Inc., for their willingness to print and circulate this book.

Gratitude is also expressed to those periodicals which first accepted the essays for publication. "Women Keep Silent in the Church" first appeared in *The Christian Bible Teacher* 17 (April 1973):138, 139, 145; "The Majority of the Men" in *What Lack We Yet?* J. D. Thomas, ed. (Abilene, Texas: Biblical Research Press, 1974), pp. 37-42; "Reflections on Preaching" in *The Harding Graduate School Bulletin* 19 (November 1979):1ff.; *The Harvester* 61 (February 1981):7-9, and *The Firm Foundation* 98 (June 1981):339; "Greek Word Studies on the Function and Authority of Preachers" in *The Firm Foundation* 97 (September 1980):567, 572, 583, 599, 615, 631, 635; "The Authority of Elders" under the title "Authority?" in *The Harding Graduate*

School of Religion Bulletin 18 (June 1978):1; "Lords Over God's Heritage?" in *The Firm Foundation* 94 (June 14, 1977):372, 379; "Greek Words for Elders," in *The Firm Foundation* 94 (June-July 1979):407, 423, 439, 455, 471, 475, 487, 491; "When God Says You Are Unworthy" in *Twentieth Century Christian* 39 (August 1977):25-27; "That Which Every Joint Supplies" in *The Firm Foundation* 91 (May 21, 1974):232; "Preaching as One Having Authority" under the title "As One Having Authority" in *The Campus Journal* 16 (Summer 1973):14-16; "Tell Us the Dream" in *The Firm Foundation* 85 (October 8, 1968):643, 645; "The Ministry of Study" in *The Campus Journal* 12 (Spring 1972):6-8, and *The Christian Bible Teacher* 15 (November 1971):368, 369, 371; "Tradition" in *The Firm Foundation* 90 (January 2, 1973):3, 12, 13; "A Self-Perpetuating Board?" in *The Firm Foundation* 99 (June 8, 1982):356, 363.

Special thanks are given to Mrs. Jean Saunders and Mrs. Jane Tomlinson, faculty secretaries, for aid in proofreading as well as in other secretarial matters. This, as all of my other works, has fewer errors because of the stylistic and other aid given by my wife, Annie May. The errors, however, are not theirs, but remain mine.

May the Lord help us to find out and to practice his will in matters of leadership as well as in all other matters.

March 1984

Jack P. Lewis

1

Women Keep Silent in the Church

The work in the church given by the Lord to women is indeed a significant one. Women ministered to the Lord of their substance (Luke 8:3); Dorcas was known for her good deeds among the widows (Acts 9:36); a husband and wife combination—Aquila and Priscilla—taught Apollos the way of the Lord more perfectly (Acts 18:26); and on repeated occasions Paul speaks of the church in their house (1 Cor. 16:19; Rom. 16:3, 4). Wherever they were, they were a center of Christian fellowship. Phoebe was a servant of the church in Cenchreae (Rom. 16:1, 2); Mary had worked among the Romans (Rom. 16:6); Tryphaena and Tryphosa labored in the Lord (16:12).

DIVISION OF LABOR

The Bible teaches that there is an equal opportunity for service to God for men and women. There is neither male nor female, but one man in Christ (Gal. 3:27, 28), but there is a division of labor. I am not able to detail in every case the specific work these women of the Bible did. Some cases are clearer than others.

A prayer meeting was held in the home of Mary in Jerusalem (Acts 12:12). Lydia supplied lodging for Paul and Silas at Philippi (Acts 16:15). The work of a Christian woman in caring for her home and her children is a work of the church. Young women are admonished to be "keepers at home" (Tit. 2:5; cf. 1 Tim. 5:4).

Our society is rapidly abandoning this ideal. The career woman is in the limelight now and with some apology a woman says, "I am just a housewife." Women abandon their homes, not because they are in need, but because they do not care for the role of a home-maker and because they want more material things. Preachers should not create an atmosphere where Christian women have guilt feelings if they are not running here and there "doing church work" while they leave their children to the maid.

Christian women are to be teachers of that which is good (Tit. 2:3). The older women are to teach younger women. The Bible does not say that this must be in private and we have no authority to rule where it has not ruled. It seems obvious also that women like Lois and Eunice (Jewish women) had implanted their faith by teaching the young man Timothy (2 Tim. 1:5). Christian women are to win their husbands to the Gospel by their reverent and chaste behavior (1 Pet. 3:2).

FEW LIMITATIONS

There are relatively few limitations in the New Testament on the work of women. By plain implication a woman could not be an elder of the church since the qualifications in 1 Timothy 3:2 say the elder is to be the "husband of one wife" and the same statement is also made in Titus 1:6. A woman could not be a deacon since the same qualification—"the husband of one wife"—is stated for the deacon (1 Tim. 3:8). Furthermore, a woman cannot be a public proclaimer of the Gospel for reasons we shall notice shortly.

1 Corinthians 14:33-36

Beyond these implications there are actually only two passages in the New Testament that place any sort of limitations on women's activities. Whatever can be said must be said from them. We will now look at these. The first is 1 Corinthians 14:33-36.

> As in all the churches of the saints the women should keep
> silence in the churches. For they are not permitted to speak,

2

but should be subordinate as even the law says. If there is anything they desire to know, let them ask their husbands at home. For it is shameful for a woman to speak in church. What! Did the word of God originate with you, or are you the only ones it has reached?

A recent article in the Memphis newspaper was entitled "St. Paul Up-dated." The various activities of women in the churches were discussed, many of them at variance with Paul's admonition.

Often it has been said that Paul, being unmarried, was just against women. But in considering the influence of Paul's attitude on the matter, we need to read one more verse: "If any one thinks that he is a prophet, or spiritual, he should acknowledge that what I am writing to you is a command of the Lord" (1 Cor. 14:37). We are not here dealing with Paul; we are dealing with "a command of the Lord." Paul also makes explicit that he is not speaking of a rule applicable only in Corinth, but "As in all the churches of the saints."

The general topic in this section of Corinthians is the exercising of spiritual gifts. Paul affirms that the spirits of the prophets are subject to the prophets (1 Cor. 14:32), that is, a person, though motivated by the Spirit, can control his speaking. Men speaking in a tongue in the church are commanded to keep silent: (a) if there is no interpreter or (b) if a revelation is given to another nearby. A woman, however, is not to speak in church at all. Paul declares that it is shameful for her to do so. Here is the most obvious place where the "Holiness" type people have always ignored and continue to ignore the plain teaching of the Bible. So-called "Neo-Pentecostalism" goes strong on speaking in tongues, but light on Paul's command of silence for women.

But is it not possible that we are dealing with a cultural problem? In Paul's culture women were in a subordinate place, but in other cultures where women are liberated, need women pay attention to Paul's charge? The majority of the commentaries affirm that they need not, and the trend of our times is to accept this idea.

It is most interesting, however, that though Paul wrote all of his letters under the inspiration of the Spirit, in this case he went out of his way as he seldom does elsewhere to say, "If anyone thinks that

3

he is a prophet, or spiritual, he should acknowledge that what I am writing to you is a command of the Lord." If the Bible has value, we are not here dealing with culture and we are not dealing with Paul alone. We are dealing with the command of the Lord. Paul appeals to the Law, likely alluding to Genesis where the woman's husband is said to rule over her (Gen. 3:16).

Hypothetical questions can be raised in objection to the plain teaching of the passage. Suppose the woman does not have a husband, whom can she ask? Now the thrust of the passage is not whom she shall ask, but that she is to keep silent. In ancient society a woman would be under the authority of her father, her brother, or her husband. I would assume (in the absence of instruction) that she could ask them or could get someone else to ask her question if need be. This question should not be an excuse to ignore the plain teaching of the passage which is silence in the churches.

Were this passage the only one to be considered, one could not make a general rule from it for the church for all time. It does deal with the exercise of spiritual gifts and these gifts are no longer present in the church. Paul speaks here of the church service; otherwise we are accusing the Spirit of contradicting itself. But even if one concludes that the passage is applicable only to spiritual gifts, there must be some reason for the prohibition.

Joel predicted that women would prophesy (Acts 2:21-29). Since 1 Corinthians 11:4, 5 envisions that women may have the gift of prophecy and may pray, and since Philip's daughters did have the gift of prophecy, yet Paul forbids women to speak in the congregation, one can only surmise that they did it in private.

1 Timothy 2:11-14

The second of the passages concerned with limitations on activities of women is 1 Timothy 2:11-14:

> Let a woman learn in silence with all submissiveness. I permit no woman to teach or to have authority over men; she is to keep silent. For Adam was formed first, then Eve; and Adam was not deceived, but the woman was deceived and became a transgressor.

4

Unlike the passage in Corinthians, this passage has no limitations as to time, place and custom. It deals with women's position in relation to men. Paul bases his command of silence and subjection upon two premises. First, woman followed Adam in creation; second, woman sinned first. Neither is a factor that time changes.

The silence *(hēsuchia)* of this passage is not the silence *(sigatō-san)* of 1 Corinthians 14:34, which means to say nothing, but is the quiet and peaceable life of 1 Timothy 2:2; the quietness of the crowd in the temple when Paul addressed them from the stairs (Acts 22:2); and the quietness with which Christians are supposed to work (2 Thess. 3:12).

In these cases it certainly does not mean that the Christian is to refrain from uttering a word. The admonition is that women not be boisterous, create confusion, or be domineering.

Teach?

At times people have read this admonition as though it said, "I permit no woman to teach," and have taken it as an absolute prohibition of any teaching. But such an interpretation creates a conflict with the instructions to Titus where women are commanded to teach women. Cannot a mother teach her children the Word of God?

Actually the sentence in Timothy has coordinate clauses and says, "I permit not a woman to teach or to usurp authority over a man." That is, "man" is the limiting factor in the two clauses. Paul is not here prohibiting women to do what he commands them to do in Titus 2 or what they are commanded to do elsewhere. He could have no intention to forbid women to sing or to forbid them to confess before men that Jesus is the Christ which they are elsewhere commanded to do. But if a woman exercises authority over men, she is in the position that Paul here forbids.

The elders of the church can ask a woman to teach other women. They can ask her to teach children. The woman who accepts such an invitation and exercises her teaching talent is not "Teaching or usurping authority over a man." She is under the oversight of and is in subjection to the elders. The elders have not discharged their task

5

of overseeing with the mere appointment of a lady to a class and leaving her to do as she pleases. They retain their responsibility to see that she teaches the truth and not error. They can do this only by knowing what she is teaching.

Preach?

But suppose the elders ask her to preach to the congregation? Could she do that? The answer is negative. Elders cannot authorize a person to do that which the Bible forbids her to do. Elders are not an autonomous authority to themselves.

I personally do not feel that a woman should lead a prayer in the church or that she should be song director if there is a man to do it.

We make a distinction between the worship services of the church at which women do not speak other than in song and in the Bible study hour. Paul in 1 Corinthians 14 speaks of "when the whole church assembles" (1 Cor. 14:23). For women his contrast is between "in the churches" (1 Cor. 14:34) and "at home" (v. 34) *(en oikō)*. It is on the basis of this distinction that in our classes women ask questions and participate in discussion. It is not "the whole church assembled." But it would be my opinion that even here a woman should not exercise authority over men.

The woman should not attempt to run the church, even behind the scenes, but should find her place of service to the Lord in the areas which He has allotted to her. Here she can without eternal danger glorify the Lord.

2

Usurp Authority?

The one occurrence of the word "usurp" in the King James Bible is in the verse 1 Timothy 2:12: "But I suffer not a woman to teach nor to usurp authority over the man, but to be in silence." According to definition, "usurp" means: "(1) to seize and hold (as office, place, powers) in possession by force without right. (2) to seize or exercise authority or possession wrongfully."

It is the second of these meanings that is ordinarily used by the English reader in exegeting the passage from Timothy. He reasons that if the elders ask a lady to do a service—of whatever nature—she is not "usurping authority" and thereby is not in danger of transgressing the Biblical instruction. What could be more normal than so to understand the word? The English reader never stops to ask if his basic premise—that "usurp" in its ordinary connotation is the crucial idea of the passage—is correct. He puts an emphasis on "usurp."

The relevant Greek phrase in this verse is *didaskein . . . oude authentein andros. Authentein* is in the N.T. only in this verse but does occur in classical authors with the meaning "to have authority, domineer over someone." The Latin Bible translated *authentein* as "domineer."

7

The ASV renders the phrase in 1 Timothy, "But I permit not a woman to teach, nor to have dominion over a man; . . ."; the RSV: ". . . to teach or to have authority over men; . . ."; the NEB: ". . . to be a teacher, nor must women domineer over men; . . ."; the NIV: ". . . to teach or to have authority over a man; . . ."; the NKJV: ". . . to teach or to have authority. . . ."

It is not the purpose of this paper to discuss the minutia of what women can and cannot scripturally do. It is to call attention to specious reasoning that is being engaged in on a concept that is not in the Greek text at all. The key phrase of this passage is not "usurp" in the sense in which it is commonly used. The key phrase is "have dominion" or "have authority."

3

The Authority of Elders

A preacher recently ventured a guess that the next division of the church is likely to be over the question of whether or not elders have authority. It struck me that if the question is being taken so seriously it would be worth a bit of checking. What does the New Testament actually say on this question, and how much of what people believe about it is deductions they have made?

The Greek word *exousia* (Latin *auctoritas* from which English "authority" comes) occurs 103 times in the New Testament and is rendered in the KJV sixty-nine times as "power"; twenty-nine times as "authority"; twice as "right"; once as "liberty"; once as "jurisdiction"; and once as "strength." The KJV also renders *epitagē* (Tit. 2:15), *huperochē* (1 Tim. 2:2), and *dunastēs* (Acts 8:27) as "authority." Furthermore, the verbal forms *exousiazō* (Luke 22:25) and *katexousiazō* (Matt. 20:25; Mark 10:42) are rendered "to exercise authority" and *authenteō* (1 Tim. 2:12) is "to usurp authority." The ASV is more consistent and renders *exousia* as "authority" fifty-nine times, including the three marginal readings (Luke 12:5; Rev. 2:6; 22:14). In two of these cases, "power," and in the third "right," are carried in the text.

The Father has his own authority (Acts 1:7). Jesus, while on earth, taught "as one having authority" (Matt. 7:29; Mark 1:23; Luke 4:32), and with "authority commanded the unclean spirits" (Mark 1:27; Luke 4:36). He had "power" on the earth to forgive sins (Matt. 9:6; Mark 2:14; Luke 5:24). His audience marveled at his authority (Luke 4:36) and glorified God who had given such authority to men (Matt. 9:8). He was challenged by the chief priests and elders, "By what authority are you doing these things, and who gave you this authority?" When they refused to answer his question about John's baptism, he refused their demand (Matt. 21:23, 24, 27; Mark 11:28, 29, 33; Luke 20:2, 8, 20). He had been given "authority to execute judgment because he is the Son of man" (John 5:27). He has authority "over all flesh" (John 17:2). He has "all power" (KJV) in heaven and on earth (Matt. 28:15). He is gone into heaven and is at the right hand of God, angels, authorities and powers being made subject to him (1 Pet. 3:22). He is exalted above all authority (Eph. 1:21). At the end of the world before rendering the kingdom up to the Father, Jesus will have put down all authority and power (1 Cor. 15:24).

When sending his disciples on the limited commission, Jesus gave them "power and authority over all demons to cure diseases" (Matt. 10:1; Mark 3:15; 6:7; Luke 9:1), and gave the seventy authority to tread on serpents (Luke 10:19). Paul, as an apostle, can speak of "our authority, which the Lord gave us for your edification, and not for your destruction" (2 Cor. 10:8). He repeats that it is authority for edification and not for destruction (2 Cor. 13:10). Titus is charged to reprove with all authority (*epitagē*; Tit. 2:15). The Christian is to pray for those in authority (*huperochē*; 1 Tim. 2:2). In one of Jesus' parables a man traveling into a far country gave authority to his servants (Mark 13:34). In the parable of the pounds the faithful servant who had gained an additional nine pounds is given authority over ten cities, and another whose pound had made five pounds was given authority over two cities (Luke 19:17).

Authority refers to civil authority; Jesus as a Galilean belonged to Herod's "jurisdiction" (*exousia*; Luke 23:7). The great ones of the earth exercise authority (Matt. 20:25; Mark 10:42). Those who have authority are called benefactors (Luke 22:25). The eunuch was a man of great authority *(dunastēs)* under Candace (Acts 8:27). Kings in the Book of Revelation receive authority (Rev. 13:17) but give it to the beast (Rev. 13:13).

Authority at times refers to military authority; the centurion Jesus encountered was a man "under authority" (Matt. 8:9; Luke 7:8). Authority at times refers to religious authority; Saul had "authority" from the chief priests to bind all those found in Damascus belonging to the Way (Acts 9:14; 26:9, 12). The devil has authority to cast into hell (Luke 12:5). The dragon, who is explained to be the devil, gave the beast in the Book of Revelation his great authority (Rev. 13:2, 4, 5); it is authority over all kindreds, tongues and nations (Rev. 13:7). The second beast has all the authority of the first beast (Rev. 17:13). The kings of the earth give their "strength" *(exousia)* to the beast (Rev. 17:13).

A Christian has the "liberty" *(exousia)* to eat meat if he chooses (1 Cor. 8:9) but is warned lest his liberty become a stumbling block to his brother. The Christian woman is to have a sign of authority on her head (1 Cor. 11:10). Those who serve at the tabernacle have no "right" (Heb. 13:10) to the altar at which Christians eat. The second death has no authority over those whose names are in the book of life (Rev. 20:6). Death was given authority in one of the scenes of the Book of Revelation over one-fourth of the earth. Those who do the Lord's commandments have a "right" *(exousia)* to the tree of life (Rev. 22:14).

The observation which strikes one strongest from this survey of *exousia* and "authority" is that though the nouns and verbs for "authority" are used for God, the devil, Jesus, the earthly rulers, the apostles, an evangelist, and even for ordinary Christians, they are never once used in connection with the discharge of the function of an elder or with the attitude the Christian is to have toward the elder. Words create the patterns in which men think. Before we divide the church over the implications of a word that does not occur in the Bible in the context with which we are differing from each other, would it not be rational to give thought to the possibility of the need for a more Biblical pattern in which to express ourselves? If we use Biblical terms we might not find ourselves so far apart after all.

4

Greek Words for Elders

INTRODUCTION

The topic, "Greek Words for Elders," is of necessity tedious and technical, and all the more so for those who have not had the privilege of mastering the Greek language. Nevertheless, it is important that we examine the Greek text in studying the question of elders. Words create the thought patterns in which men can think. There is not a one-to-one equivalence in translation from Greek into English. Since most words have more than one meaning, the English word chosen by the translator may have some overtones quite foreign to the Greek word the original writer used; and where so, it is easy for men to take off on those overtones and thereby to expound ideas the Bible never taught. On the opposite side of the problem, the Greek word may be richer in connotation than the English word. In such cases dependence on the English word alone robs us of concepts we need.

I. NOUNS

In considering the Greek words for elders, we first have implications of a series of nouns to consider: *presbuteros, episkopos, poimēn, didaskalos,* and *oikonomos.*

These Greek words have given us in English the three pairs of words—pastor and shepherd, bishop and overseer, elder and presbyter—together with two other words not so closely related to each other: teacher and steward. All are variant designations emphasizing aspects of the service of one group of men.

Presbuteroi (elders) of Ephesus are called to Miletus and informed by Paul that they have been made *episkopoi* (overseers) in order to *poimainein* (shepherd) the church of God (Acts 20:17ff.). All three roots are here used for one group of people. Furthermore, Titus is in Crete to appoint *presbuteroi* (elders), but is given the qualifications of *episkopoi* (overseers) who are said to be God's *oikonomoi* (stewards; Tit. 1:5-7). Paul proceeds to point out that the *presbuteros* (elder) must be blameless and also that the *episkopos* (overseer) must be blameless—they are the same individual. The *presbuteroi* (elders) are to *poimainein* (shepherd) the *poimnion tou theou* ("the flock of God"); and if the less well attested textual variant of the passage is followed, they are also to be *episkopountes* ("exercising the oversight"; 1 Pet. 5:1, 2). These three references should be adequate to make clear that in our terms we have one service with multiple aspects.

Didascalos

In Ephesians 4:11, in a list of gifts, Paul states that there are some "shepherds and teachers" (*didaskaloi*). The structure of this sentence should be noticed. Paul precedes each item in the list with the words *tous de* ("some") until he comes to the last two, where there is only one particle for the two, suggesting that they are to be taken, not as two, but as one. In English, then, one does not translate, "some shepherds, and some teachers." I would not deduce from the statement that some elders should be shepherds and that others should be teachers, but that these functions are to be combined in the elder.

While it is recognized that Ephesians 4:11 deals with "gifts" in the church, that the elder should be a teacher in an age where the gifts have ceased is further made clear in his qualification "able to

14

teach" (*didaktikos*; 1 Tim. 3:2). It is underscored by Titus: "He must hold firmly to the trustworthy message as it has been taught, so that he can encourage others by sound doctrine and refute those who oppose it" (Tit. 1:9). Furthermore, it is said that the elder who "labors in preaching and teaching" (1 Tim. 5:17) is "worthy of double honor." "Teacher" is by no means used exclusively for elders in the N.T. Quite the contrary! The Epistle to the Hebrews (5:12) reminds us that in time all Christians should become teachers. Nothing is said in the N.T. about elders being in the church in Antioch, but they had teachers (Acts 13:1).

The term "teacher" should remind us that the church is essentially a school. Its members are "pupils" or "disciples" *(mathetēs)*. Jesus is the "one teacher" (*didaskalos*; Matt. 23:8); but under him there are other teachers, and among these are the elders. If one is to teach, he must, himself, know. The teacher concept is most provocative for how the elder should conceive of his function and how the people should regard him. Is not the church a school and the eldership its instructors?

The context of Matthew 23:8 makes clear that the designation "teacher" is not to be regarded as a term of exaltation. There is "one teacher." The disciples are "brethren" *(adelphoi)*. Furthermore, those things said about the family qualification of the elder and those things said about his being "an example" make clear that his teaching is not of the "do as I say, and not as I do" sort. He teaches by what he has been, by what he is now, by what he does, and by what he says.

Oikonomos

Oikonomos, meaning "steward," "one given a trust," or "manager," occurs in nine N.T. passages. It designates the owner's representative in the absentee landlord parables (Luke 12:42; 16:1, 3, 8); the steward of a city (Rom. 16:23); and the steward in charge of a child (Gal. 4:2). In spiritual matters it designates the apostles as "stewards of God" (1 Cor. 4:1, 2); and designates each Christian as a steward of God's varied grace (1 Pet. 4:10).

This term occurs once describing the elder. He must, as God's steward, be blameless (Tit. 1:7). *Oikonomos* designates the elder as God's representative in the matters God had in mind for him, but does not specifically indicate within itself what type of leadership he is to exercise. It makes quite clear that his position or service is not an autonomous one; he is not a legislator; he is not a law unto himself. He is accountable to God and is under God. Furthermore, as Paul said about his own position (1 Cor. 4:1, 2), as a steward he must be faithful in his stewardship.

Looking at this same term from the people's viewpoint, we see that the rabbinic rule, "A man's representative is as the man himself,"[1] is quite applicable. The elder is to the people God's representative. One must be impressed with how the terms used for elders are two-edged swords. They are humbling so that the possessor has no grounds for boasting; yet they are exalting, demanding recognition on the part of those led. The elder is only a steward; yet to those led, he is "God's steward."

Elder

The Greek word *presbutēs*, meaning "an old man," occurs three times in the Greek New Testament. Zechariah says, "I am an old man" (Luke 1:18); Paul admonishes Titus that older men are to be temperate (Tit. 2:2); and then describes himself as "Paul the aged" (Philem. 9). The feminine form occurs once. Paul admonishes that older women (*presbutis*) are to be reverent (Tit. 2:3).

The adjective *presbuteros*, the comparative form of *presbutēs*, occurs in the N.T. in a variety of senses. In six passages it designates those born first: "the elder son" (Luke 15:25); "from the eldest" (John 8:9); "your old men" (Acts 2:17); "older men" (1 Tim. 5:1), and in the feminine form, "an older woman" (1 Tim. 5:2); and then finally occurs in 1 Peter 5:5 where the younger are to submit to the elder—a statement open to dispute whether the admonition holds for every older person or should be listed with those passages dealing with Christian leaders. Likely it is the former of these since in the passage the contrasts, "younger," "the older ones," "one another" and a general admonition to submission are set forth. Likely when the writer of the two Epistles of John designates himself as "the elder" (2 John 1; 3 John 1) the meaning is "an older man."

Presbuteros also occurs four times designating those people who have gone before. There are the traditions of the elders (Matt. 15:2; Mark 7:3, 5); and there are the "men of old" (Heb. 11:2) who have received divine approval.

In twenty-five additional verses (including parallel passages) *presbuteros* designates Jewish leaders, most often occurring in the phrases "chief priest, elders, and scribes," or in "chief priests and elders" (Matt. 16:21; Mark 8:31; Luke 9:22; Matt. 21:32; Mark 11:27; Luke 20:1; Matt. 26:3; Mark 14:43; Matt. 26:57; Mark 14:53; Matt. 27:1; Mark 15:1; Matt. 27:3, 12, 41; 28:12; Luke 7:3; 22:52; Acts 4:5, 8, 23; 23:14; 25:15; 24:1).

In twelve cases in the Apocalypse *presbuteros* designates figures in heaven (Rev. 4:4, 10; 5:5, 6, 8, 11, 14; 7:11, 13; 11:16; 14:3; 19:4).

In sixteen instances (seventeen if 1 Pet. 5:5 should be included) *presbuteros* designates Christian leaders. To the elders of Jerusalem the charity of the early church was brought (Acts 11:30); elders were appointed by Paul and Barnabas in the churches (Acts 14:23); those of Jerusalem joined in the circumcision discussion and decision along with the apostles and the whole church (Acts 15:2, 4, 6, 22, 23; 16:4). The elders of Ephesus were called to Miletus (Acts 20:17); and those of Jerusalem, along with James, were greeted by Paul when he returned from the third journey (Acts 21:18). Paul admonishes that the elders who direct the affairs of the church well (*kalōs proestōtes*) deserve double honor (1 Tim. 5:17); Titus is to appoint elders in Crete (Tit. 1:5). The elders of the church are to be called in for the sick (James 5:14); and Peter as a fellow elder (*sumpresbuteros*) admonishes the elders (1 Pet. 5:1).

That there was a plurality of elders in each congregation is obvious. There was such in Jerusalem (Acts 11:30; 15:2, 6, 22; 21:18). Paul and Barnabas appointed elders in each church (Acts 14:23; Ephesus (Acts 20:17) and Philippi (Phil. 1:1) had a plurality; and Titus is left in Crete to appoint elders in every church (Tit. 1:5). 1 Clement shows that the plurality continued in Corinth into

17

the second century; and Polycarp shows the same for Philippi and Smyrna (see also Acts 15:4; 1 Tim. 4:14, 5:17; James 5:14; 1 Pet. 5:1).[2] The term is never used in the N.T. in the singular number when any duty pertaining to the office is described.

The Greek noun *presbuterion*, designating the discharging of the function of the elder, is three times in the N.T.: twice for Jewish gatherings in the phrases, "the assembly of the elders of the people gathered . . ." (Luke 22:66), and "the council of the elders" (Acts 22:5). Then *presbuterion* occurs once for a Christian group. Timothy had received his gift when the elders laid hands on him (1 Tim. 4:14). The KJV, ASV, and NASV render this passage "the laying on of hands of the presbytery"; the RSV, "the elders"; but the NIV uses "the body of elders." As McGarvey recognized,[3] the English of this term could be the "eldership."

The fact that *presbuteros* is used both in its technical meaning for a leader of the church, and yet retains its ordinary meaning of an old man, leaves doubt in a few passages over which sense is meant. Though all of us are accustomed to the use of 1 Peter 5:5 as a demand for submission to the elders, it is quite likely that the passage is a general admonition to submission in which the elders would be included as older men along with other old men rather than exclusively dealing with the elders. If one notices the context, he has the younger ones (*neōteroi*) subject to the older ones (*presbuteroi*) and then "all" (*pantes*) clothing themselves with humility toward "one another" (*allēlois*). The passage is a general call to humility. This same sort of problem is also encountered in 1 Timothy 5:1 when the admonition, "Do not rebuke an older man (elder?),"[4] is followed by talk of behavior toward young men, older women, younger women, and widows. Then the shift is again at verse 17 to *presbuteroi* which all agree are "elders."

The etymology of the term *presbuteros*, as well as the qualifications set forth in both Timothy and Titus, points to leadership by men of seniority, prominence, experience, and wisdom. *Presbuteros*, though meaning "older man," does not occur in the N.T. in the derogatory sense of "senility." A specific age for such a person is not given; and age alone does not qualify one. One cannot be appointed to be an old man; time takes care of that. The elder is not to be a new convert (*neophutos*; 1 Tim. 3:6). Paul and Barnabas (Acts 14:23; *cheirotonein*) and Titus (Tit. 1:5; *kathistanai*) appointed men to be elders in the churches. The term elder, therefore, must be understood as an official designation for a service to which one is appointed. Its etymology and the qualifications show the fallacy of designating boys in their teen years as "elders" and reflect unfavorably on the practice of an earlier generation of the Restoration Movement when every preacher was called "elder," somewhat like every preacher is now "brother." The qualifications for elders eliminate women from service.

When we search beyond the obvious etymological meaning of *presbuteros*—that kind of older, experienced man—for insight into the position and function of such persons, we are at first drawn to the O.T. world. Among Israel's neighbors were groups of "elders." The Egyptians (Gen. 50:7), the Moabites and the Midianites (Num. 22:7), and the Greeks (*Iliad* 1:490; 4:225) had them. Among the Hittites, elders administered municipal functions and settled local disputes.[5] In Mesopotamian documents from the eighteenth to the eighth centuries B.C., "elders" are seen as the people's representatives and defenders, though without administrative functions.[6] In the Amarna Letters, a Phoenician town Irkata had its "elders."[7]

In ancient Israel, before the time of Moses, leadership functions were exercised by *zekenim* ("elders"; Ex. 3:16; 4:29; 19:7; 24:1, 9); then Moses selected seventy elders in the desert to aid him (Num. 11:24). The elders of Israel laid their hands on the sacrificial animal (Lev. 4:15); exercised judicial functions (Deut. 25:7); approved the reign of a king (2 Sam. 5:3); and were advisers of the king (1 Kings 20:8). They cooperated with Elijah against the king (2 Kings 6:32) and they interfered in the trial of Jeremiah (Jer. 26:17).

There were also elders of a tribe (Deut. 31:28; Judg. 11:5; 1 Sam. 30:26; 2 Sam. 19:11; 2 Kings 23:1); and there were elders of a city (Judg. 8:14; 1 Kings 21:8; 2 Kings 10:5; Ezra 10:14) who had the power of life and death, responsible for delivering the murderer to the avenger of blood (Deut. 19:21; Josh. 20:4); for cleansing the city where a murdered man was found (Deut. 21:4); for giving the death sentence on the rebellious son (Deut. 21:19-21); for hearing the case where a man slandered the virginity of his bride (Deut. 22:15); and of hearing cases involving technicalities of rejected levirate marriage (Deut. 25:8).

Jewish elders are frequently encountered in the N.T. One segment of the Sanhedrin is so designated (Luke 22:66; Acts 22:5),[8] but it is usually to the synagogue and its organization that scholars turn for a pattern for the elders of the church. The synagogue elders (Luke 7:3 and the Theodotus synagogue inscription)[9] are thought usually to have been identical with the elders of the town.[10] Their function was judicial and administrative. They had no responsibility for the worship of the synagogue, for the custody of right doctrine, or for the exposition of Scripture. According to surviving inscriptions, among Jews the title may have been honorific at times, even held by women.

There were also elders in the Hellenistic towns of both Egypt and Asia Minor with varied functions.[11]

Actually, the early church seems little influenced—other than sharing a common term—by these other groups. It is precarious to reason that early Jewish Christians would most likely have taken over the functions of the elders they knew in the synagogue or that Gentile Christians would have taken the function of elders in the Hellenistic cities as their pattern for the function of elders in the churches. The civil and judicial functions of the Jewish elders are not in the forefront in the work laid out for the elders in the N.T.

On the other hand, the pastoral function of Christian elders was not the task of Jewish elders of either the city or the synagogue. Sharing a term does not mean sharing the function. Christianity shared the use of the term "priest" with the Jews and the Greeks, but the function is vastly different. It is fallacious to transfer the concept of the position of an elder drawn from the various areas to N.T. teaching about the eldership—just as fallacious as the practice of a congregation in Detroit whose elders act as if they were automobile corporation executives, or of a group of elders in a democracy who conceive of themselves as the Senate or the House of Representatives.

The term "elder" suggests a leadership built on respect and reverence (cf. Lev. 19:32), a reverence that recognizes ability, service, knowledge, example, and seniority. An elder, some time ago, said to me, "I do what my doctor tells me, not because he has 'authority' over me, but because I respect his professional judgment." I, myself, am quite happy to follow my wife in those areas where I think she knows more than I do; but she does not have organic authority over me.

Christians are taught to remember their leaders and to imitate their faith (Heb. 13:7). They are to regard those over them highly in love because of their works (1 Thess. 5:13). If one wishes to call this position one of "moral authority," for communication purposes, I might grant the term despite the absence of the use of the term "authority" to describe the position of elders in the New Testament as I pointed out in a previous article.[12]

Elders are not autonomous. They are "undershepherds" (the word is not in the N.T.), and Jesus is the "chief shepherd." Though we today may argue that elders are to be obeyed in matters of opinion, no informed person in the church believes that elders are to be arbitrarily obeyed without regard to where they lead. Under the heat of argument some may conceive that they differ from others on this point, but in the end they have to grant that they too draw or would draw a line.

Hence the point of discussion should not be whether elders should be obeyed or not—the Bible explicitly and plainly teaches that they should be (Heb. 13:17; I assume that the leaders are elders)—but the question is, obeyed in what and for what reason?

If the elders lead the congregation into the use of instrumental music (as they did in some cases two generations ago), are they to be followed? If they forbid the support of orphans' homes, are they to be followed? If they denounce congregational cooperation, are they to be heeded? If they rule that ladies should not attend worship in pantsuits, should they expect to be heeded? If they rule that only the KJV is to be read, are they acting within their proper function?

Just where is the clear line between where elders should expect to be followed and not followed?

We all agree that the position of an elder is not comparable to that of an officer in the army. The centurion said of himself, "I say to one 'Go,' and he goes; and to another 'Come,' and he comes; and to my slave, 'Do this,' and he does it" (Luke 7:8). The position of the congregation toward the elders is not that described in "The Charge of the Light Brigade": "Theirs not to reason why; theirs but to do and die." Neither is the position of the elder comparable to that of the judge who (as a representative of the state) has the power of life and death. We are therefore all brought back to the question of the boundaries of responsibility.

Generalizations do not fit all cases, but in some of our congregations men have been designated elders whose primary qualifications beyond ordinary Christian character are that they are pleasant, outgoing personalities, are successful businessmen who can make large contributions, and are men who have the confidence of a segment of the people. In their congregations are other men that are older than they are, have been in the church longer than they have, know more about the Bible than they do, and have more skill and experience in teaching the Bible than they do. Where are the boundaries of relationship of these two peoples?

But one says, "I mean that 'qualified elders' are to be submitted to." Again we are back to a relative question. Who is to sit in judgment on whether an elder is qualified or not? If you say, "The congregation," then we are reminded that there are no elders the congregation has not appointed. This would mean that all are qualified—but are they?

If you say, "Well, the individual forms his own opinion on that question"—then we are in the situation where elders are qualified when I like their opinions and not when I do not; qualified when they hire me but perhaps not when they fire me. Who has ever been fired that did not question the judgment of those who did it?

Overseer

The noun *episkopos*, derived from the root *episkeptomai* (to oversee), less frequently used in the N.T. than is *presbuteros*,

22

occurs only five times.[13] Once it denotes our Savior—"the Shepherd and Bishop of your souls" (1 Pet. 2:25). In using "Bishop" for *episkopos*, the KJV translated the term in the light of Christian history. But in the light of its rich Greek and Jewish background, *episkopos* in combination with *poimēn* says a great deal. Jesus is the one who has the fullest knowledge of souls.

Episkopos is four times used for leaders of the churches (Acts 20:28; Phil. 1:1; 1 Tim. 3:2; Tit. 1:7). The KJV used both "overseer" (Acts 20:28) and "bishop" (Phil. 1:1; 1 Tim. 3:2; Tit. 1:1; 1 Pet. 2:25) as its rendering of this term. The ASV consistently used "bishop" in the text of all the passages, but listed "overseer" in the margin; then the RSV used "guardian" in Acts 20:28 and in 1 Peter 2:25, but used "bishop" in the other cases.

The NIV has reversed the practice of the ASV and put "overseer" in the text and "bishop" in the margin in all cases. This reversal is necessary in view of the connotation "bishop" has taken on in current religious usage. The Scripture is not speaking of the bishop in the denominational sense of a man over a group of churches. "Overseer" corresponds to the etymology of the Greek word and avoids the erroneous connotation that may be attached to "bishop."

A related noun, *episkopē*, occurs four times, twice in the sense of "visitation" (Luke 19:44: "time of your visitation"; 1 Pet. 2:12: "day of visitation"); once for the position among the apostles (KJV: "bishoprick"; ASV and RSV: "office"; NIV: "place of leadership") vacated by Judas (Acts 1:20). Then *episkopē* is once (1 Tim. 3:1) for the role the church leader fills.[14] To desire this service is to desire, not an eminent position, but "a good work."

Prior to its use in the Pastoral letter, *episkopē* had established itself in the Septuagint as a term of office (Num. 4:16; Ps. 108:8). From the time of William Tyndale through the RSV *episkopē* is rendered "the office of a bishop"; but in the NIV is rendered as "being an overseer" and in the GNB as "to be a church leader." McGarvey thought the term should be "overseership."[15]

The related verbal form, *episkopein*, occurs once (Heb. 12:15) in an undisputed text but is not there technically dealing with church leadership. This participial form is rendered: KJV: "looking diligently"; ASV: "looking carefully"; RSV and NIV: "see to it." Then, *episkopein* occurs in a textual variant in 1 Peter 5:2 which carries square brackets in the UBS Greek text, but which is listed only in the apparatus of the Nestle text and is not included in the text at all. Though carried in the KJV as "taking the oversight *thereof*," and from that source becoming a favorite prooftext of those who use that version and discuss the eldership; and though carried in the NIV as "serving as overseers" without notation that it is a variant, the diligent student of God's Word cannot hold this reading as a certainty.

The problem is discussed in the *Textual Commentary on the Greek New Testament*[16] where it is pointed out that the reading is supported by P[72], by the corrector of Sinaiticus, by Alexandrinus, and by most other witnesses, but is absent in the original hand of Sinaiticus, Vaticanus, Ms. 33, and other witnesses. The balance of evidence seems to merit its inclusion in the text; but its doubtful authenticity demands that it be enclosed in brackets. The RSV relegated the reading to the footnotes, and the NASV omits it without notation. One must be careful that he is not building his doctrine on textual variants merely because he prefers the way the variants fit his pattern of thought.

Episkopos was used in secular Greek for various types of overseership—religious and non-religious. The gods were *episkopoi* who watched over men or things. When applied to men, "protective care" is at the heart of the activity. The *episkopoi* were often local officials or officers of the societies, but the term is never used with precision.[17] The term was used in the Septuagint for God (Job 20:29; Is. 60:17) and for the army chief (Num. 31:14; 2 Kings 11:15), for magistrates, and for other services (Num. 4:16; Neh. 11:9, 14, 22). The *episkopos* is an intermediary below the supreme power, but is over the people, acting in behalf of that supreme power in relation to the people. The various usages do not form a clear model on which the Christian *episkopē* was formed.

The exact nature of the work of the *episkopos* is not implied in the term itself. The term is never used in the N.T. for the charismatic leadership of the church. The responsibility of the *episkopos* is described in terms of *poimainein* ("to shepherd"; Acts 20:28)—his is a watchful, solicitous direction of the congregation. The point of the office was service, and service alone.[18]

A memory of fifty years in the Lord's church gives me an ample supply of examples in which we preachers identified our preferences with the will of God and defined the Christian life in terms of no coffee, no Cokes, no movies, no card playing, definition of length of hair and of style of dress. I might as well confess that because of the conditioning I have not yet completely escaped from the momentary pangs of conscience at the suggestion of a good game of Rook. Perhaps then "overseers" are not greater sinners when they too have fallen into the same snares and have attempted to bring the congregation into line with their preferences on matters on which the Lord has not spoken. Is it not fair to say that the overseer, as far as his work with the congregation is concerned, is overseer of God's will, and not the imposer of his own will?

Shepherd

The verb *poimainein* occurs in eleven N.T. passages; twice in the literal meaning of "keeping sheep" (Luke 17:7; 1 Cor. 9:7); four times (Matt. 2:6; Rev. 7:17; 12:5; 19:15) for the role of leadership exercised by Jesus over God's people; once (Rev. 2:27) for the position held by him who overcomes—like Jesus, he is said to "rule the nations with a rod of iron"—once for the responsibility to which Peter is called (John 21:16), "feed my sheep"; once for the troublemakers "who look after themselves" (Jude 12); then, twice it depicts the work of the leadership in the church. In our translations it is rendered: "to feed the church of God" (Acts 20:28) and "Tend the flock of God that is your charge" (1 Pet. 5:2).

The noun *poimēn* (shepherd) occurs in seventeen N.T. passages. In four passages (Luke 2:8, 15, 18, 20) concerned with the birth narratives, it denotes the literal occupation of tending sheep; it is twice (Matt. 9:36; Mark 6:34) in the figurative expression where the people are compared to "sheep not having a shepherd"; twice in the saying (Matt. 26:31; Mark 14:27) "strike the shepherd and the sheep will be scattered"; and once in the judgment of people being separated as a shepherd separates sheep and goats (Matt. 25:32). However, *poimēn* occurs most frequently in depicting the relationship of Jesus to his people, first in the allegory of the shepherd of the Fourth Gospel. The one who enters by the door is the "shepherd of the sheep" (John 10:2); "I am the good shepherd" (John 10:11, 14); the one who is not the shepherd flees when the wolf comes (John 10:12); the good shepherd lays down his life for the sheep; there will be "one flock, one shepherd" (John 10:16). Then, Christ is the great shepherd of the sheep (Heb. 13:20); and Christian people have returned to "the Shepherd and Guardian" of their souls (1 Pet. 2:25). Christ is the "chief shepherd" (*archipoimēn*; 1 Pet. 5:4).

Besides these various passages, *poimēn* also occurs for the leader of God's people (Eph. 4:11); but there is traditionally rendered "pastor"—"some pastors and teachers." The term "pastor" is the Latin term for "shepherd." However, using "shepherd" as the rendering in Ephesians 4:11 (as is done in the other occurrences of *poimēn*) avoids the error attached to "pastor" by denominational usage which makes the pastor the preacher.

The comparison of the leader of men to a shepherd has a challenging and interesting Middle Eastern background. In an Amarna letter, Abdiheba, the ruler of Jerusalem, describes himself as "I am a shepherd of the king."[19] A Nimrud building slab by Adad-nirari declares of a ruler, "He whose shepherding they made (to be) as good for the people as (is) the plant of life and whose throne they founded securely."[20]

In Hebrew, *ro'eh* is a noun coming from the verb meaning "to pasture" or "tend" a flock, designating many O.T. figures beginning with Abel (Gen. 4:2). Included are Abraham, Isaac, Jacob, and Jacob's sons (Gen. 13:7; 26:20; 30:36; 37:12ff.). Moses (Ex. 3:1), David (1 Sam. 16:11ff.), and Amos (Amos 1:1) were shepherding sheep when God called them. God communicated to a people who knew shepherding the idea that he was the Shepherd of Israel. Jacob spoke of "the God who has led [KJV, "fed"] me all my life long to this day" (Gen. 48:15). But the idea was unforgettably expounded by David in the twenty-third Psalm and in Psalms 78:70; 95:7; 100:3. It was also used by Asaph in Psalms 77:20; 80:1: "Give ear, O Shepherd of Israel, thou who leadest Joseph like a flock." The idea is further elaborated by Isaiah (Is. 40:11); Jeremiah (Jer. 31:10); Ezekiel (Ezek. 34:12); Micah (Mic. 2:12); and Zechariah (Zech. 11:4). In each of these instances it is the guiding and protecting—not the domineering or ruling—of the flock that is stressed.

In keeping with the comparison, one finds in many O.T. passages that the leaders of God's people are spoken of as shepherds under God. Without leaders, the people are compared to sheep without a shepherd (Num. 27:17; 1 Kings 22:17); but the prophets, priests, and kings who had failed God's people were condemned as shepherds who had deserted or abused the flock (Jer. 2:8; 10:21; 23:1ff.; Ezek. 34:2ff.).

The shepherd metaphor cannot be understood apart from the related one which uses "flock: *poimnē* or *poimnion*" for the congregation. This metaphor is abundantly used in the O.T. from the time of Hosea (4:16) where we encounter the expressions, "Jehovah's flock" (Jer. 13:17) and "the flock of his pasture" (Ps. 95:7). It is continued in the Apocrypha (Sirach 18:13) and the Pseudepigrapha, particularly in Ethiopic *Enoch* (83-90) and the *Songs of Solomon* (17:40).

In the N.T. *poimnē* ("flock") occurs in four cases; once used literally for the flock of shepherds (Luke 2:8); once in the O.T. quotation: "the sheep of the flock will be scattered" (Matt. 26:31); once when Jesus predicts that with the bringing in of other sheep [the Gentiles] there will be one flock (John 10:16); and finally, once in Paul: "Who tends a flock without getting some of the milk?" (1 Cor. 9:7).

Poimnion (the diminutive of *poimnē*) is also in four N.T. passages. Jesus spoke of his disciples as "little flock" (Luke 12:32); the bishops are to take heed to the flock (Acts 20:28) and are warned that the arising wolves would not spare the flock (Acts 20:29); and elders are "to shepherd" the "flock of God" (1 Pet. 5:2).

The same metaphor also lies back of those cases where God's

27

people are said to be "sheep" *(probaton)*. The O.T. speaks of "the sheep of his pasture" (Ps. 95:7; cf. 74:1; 79:13; 100:3; Jer. 23:1; Ezek. 34:31); "The sheep of your [God's] possession" (Mic. 7:14), and of "my sheep" (Jer. 23:2f.). Taking up this figure, Jesus describes his mission, and that of his disciples on the "limited commission," as "to the lost sheep of the house of Israel" (Matt. 10:6, 15:24); he saw crowds as "sheep not having a shepherd" (Matt. 9:36; cf. Num. 27:17). In a sense the metaphor of sheep and shepherd covers all lost people; but there is also a more restricted use of it for those belonging to the Lord which is expounded in the repeated occurrences of the term in the allegory of John 10 and which lies behind the judgment parable where men are separated as sheep and goats (Matt. 25:32, 33). This term is of infrequent occurrence outside the Gospels. Paul speaks of being accounted as sheep for the slaughter (Rom. 8:36); the writer of the Epistle to the Hebrews speaks of Jesus being the great shepherd of the sheep (Heb. 13:20); and Peter speaks of our straying like sheep but returning to the Shepherd of our souls (1 Pet. 2:25).

One cannot legitimately hang on a Biblical metaphor whatever idea chances into his fertile imagination. The impact of a metaphor is limited to the concept the user of it had in view. The shepherd had the power of life and death over the sheep. He could sell a sheep, he could hit a wayward one over the nose with his rod if he chose, he could slaughter one; but to deduce that the shepherd metaphor implies that the elder has such power is an obvious fallacy. What are the motifs Biblical writers call on in this metaphor?

First, the relation of the shepherd and the sheep is a relation built on trust. "The sheep hear his voice, and he calls his own sheep by name and leads them out" (John 10:3). There is a personal concern and care for the sheep. In our congregations where the shepherd looks over the departing congregation and comments, "I do not know all these people," this relation has broken down. In situations known to me where some prominent elders over a period of twenty years have never been in the home of members who attend regularly—not even at the time of death in the family, nor have had the members in theirs—the shepherd relation is lacking.

28

The seeking of the lost is another motif of the shepherd metaphor. Ezekiel said, "The weak you have not strengthened, the sick you have not healed, the crippled you have not bound up, the strayed you have not brought back, the lost you have not sought, and with force and harshness you have ruled them" (Ezek. 34:4). Jesus pictured the masses as sheep having no shepherd (Matt. 9:36), and his unforgettable picture of the shepherd leaving the ninety-nine in the fold to seek the lost one (Matt. 18:12-14; Luke 15:3-6) underscores the metaphor in a challenging way.

The shepherding of the flock is a part of the shepherd image. The verb *poimainein* occurs eleven times in the N.T., but the force is obscured because the KJV rendered it seven times as "feed," and four times as "rule." The term in reality expresses the entire work of the shepherd in caring for his flock—not just feeding. This verb occurs in the N.T. for the literal caring for the sheep (Luke 17:7; 1 Cor. 9:7); occurs in a metaphor for a ruler (Matt. 2:6); occurs in the Lord's charge to Peter where there is an alternation of verbs between "feed" (John 21:15, 17) and "care for" (John 21:16): "feed my lambs/sheep"; and then occurs twice for the work of the elder. First, Paul told the elders of Ephesus "to feed" *(poimainein)* the church of God (Acts 20:28). Then the other occurrence is the command "Feed the flock of God which is your charge" (1 Pet. 5:2). In contrast with this work, the evildoers of the book of Jude "feed themselves" (v. 12) as also do the condemned shepherds of the book of Ezekiel (Ezek. 34). The Lamb will be shepherd of the victorious (Rev. 7:17); then in three passages the Lord threatens "to rule" (shepherd) the wicked with a rod of iron (Rev. 2:27; 12:5; 19:15). Teaching is a part of shepherding; but shepherding is not completely discharged by teaching lessons.

Yet again it was the task of the shepherd to guard the sheep from thieves (John 10:1, 8, 10) and from wild beasts (Matt. 10:16; Luke 10:3; John 10:12; Acts 20:29). David spoke of his confronting the lion and the bear (1 Sam. 17:34). Against these dangers the shepherd was always armed: "Thy rod and thy staff, they comfort me," said David (Ps. 23:4). "Those who tend sheep must fight the wolf." The elder as shepherd has the task of safeguarding the flock from "grievous wolves" that arise both from within and from without (Acts 20:29, 30).

Then there is the sacrificing of self for the sheep: "The good shepherd lays down his life for the sheep" (John 10:11). While in its setting this statement is an allusion to the approaching death of Jesus; and while the elder is not called on literally to die for the flock; the shepherd image does suggest a sacrificial life for the flock rather than a life for self.

In the discharging of these various functions, the shepherd has first his own example. "He goes before them and the sheep follow him" (John 10:4). He is to be an "example to the flock" (1 Pet. 5:3). One is reminded that Jesus began "to do and to teach" (Acts 1:1); and Ezra to study, to do and to teach (Ezra 7:10). But included in the shepherding is the teaching of the Word "which is able to build up" and which "gives an inheritance among all those who are sanctified" (Acts 20:32). In Palestinian shepherding the shepherd leads the sheep; he does not drive them. If we should move from the "board of directors" mindset in our congregations and create a situation in which the shepherd is leading sheep who know his voice, of their being shepherded, and of shepherds ready to lay down their lives for the sheep, there would be much more willingness of the sheep to follow than we sometimes encounter.

II. VERBS

Our topic also requires that we give consideration to two verbs—*proistēmi* and *hēgeisthai*.

Proistēmi

A recent college lectureship had listed as one of its topics for discussion, "Do Elders Rule?" I did not hear the address and have no way to know what position the speaker took; but if one accepts the KJV as final authority, indeed elders do rule! That version translated *proistēmi* as "rule" five times (Rom. 12:8; 1 Tim. 3:4, 5, 12; 5:17) and also rendered *hēgeisthai* as "rule" in Hebrews 13:7, 17, and 24. If, however, one asks what the concept "rule" automatically suggests to him and then asks if that is really the position elders hold to the church, he might have a modified opinion. If he

30

asks what concept *proistēmi* should convey, and what *hēgeisthai* should convey, he might also have a modified opinion.

In its eight occurrences in the N.T., *proistēmi* occurs only in intransitive forms, and according to Kittel's *Theological Diction-ary*[21] has the sense of "to lead" but in each case the context forces one to consider the meaning "to care for." Hence, Romans 12:8, which the KJV rendered "He who ruleth with diligence," has the meaning from the context, "He who cares with zeal." That is, the possessors of this gift have the primary task of caring for others. 1 Thessalonians 5:12 calls for respect for those who work hard among you, who care for you in the Lord, and who admonish you. Kittel's *Theological Dictionary* comments, "the task of the *prois-tamenous* is in large measure that of pastoral care, and the empha-sis is not on their rank or authority but on their efforts for the eternal salvation of believers."[22]

Hort wrote in *The Christian Ecclesia,*

> The word was usually applied to informal leadership and management of all kinds rather than to definite offices and was associated with the services rendered to dependents by a patron (cf. Rom. 12:8), so that (as in Romans) helpful leader-ship in Divine things would be approximately the thought suggested.[23]

In 1 Timothy 3:4-5, the one who cares for *(proistamenon)* his own house is the one who can care for *(epimelēsetai)* the church of God. *Epimelēsetai* is elsewhere in the N.T. only used for the care of the wounded man by the Samaritan and the innkeeper (Luke 10:34, 35). There is a challenging sidelight on the elder's care of the church in this word. Until I began this study I had always understood 1 Timothy 3:5 in administrative terms. Deacons also are those who care well *(proistamenoi)* for their own houses (1 Tim. 3:12). Kittel's *Theological Dictionary* grants that the authority of the head of the household *(patria potestates)* is in view but urges that "his attention is primarily directed, not to the exercise of power, but to the discretion and care to be shown therein."[24]

Of 1 Timothy 5:17, *The Theological Dictionary of the New*

Testament comments,

> The context shows that the reference is not merely to elders who rule well, but especially to those who exercise a sincere cure of souls. The second half of the verse makes their diligence in pastoral care the criterion.[25]

This concept of the elders' work and position is fully in keeping with Jesus' statement, "the one who would be chief *(ho hēgoumenos)* is to be as he who serves" (Luke 22:26). It fits the picture gained from Phoebe who is "patroness" or "protector" *(prostatis)* of Paul and others (cf. 1 Clem. 36:1; 61:3; 64:1, where the term is used in masculine form for Jesus). Despite the use of the same verb stem which is used for the position of elders, one would certainly not argue that this woman had "authority" over Paul and the others in the sense "authority" is usually understood. In the sense of "devoting oneself to," *proistēmi* occurs twice for every Christian. He is to devote himself to good works (Tit. 3:8, 14).

Hēgeisthai

Hēgeisthai as a participle, meaning "to lead" or "to guide," and as a finite verb, often meaning "to account," occurs twenty-five times in the New Testament.

In the meaning "esteem" or "think oneself" (Acts 26:2; 2 Cor. 9:5; Phil. 2:25); or "account" (Phil. 2:3, 6; 3:7, 8), the term describes activities of Christians. The disobedient is not to be esteemed as an enemy (2 Thess. 3:15). Jesus "counted" Paul faithful (1 Tim. 1:12); slaves are to esteem their masters worthy of honor (1 Tim. 6:1). One can count the blood of the covenant common (Heb. 10:29). Sarah considered God faithful (Heb. 11:11) and Moses counted the reproach of Christ greater than the treasures of Egypt (Heb. 11:26). Christians are to count temptations joy (James 1:2). Peter "thinks it right" (2 Pet. 1:13); false teachers "count it pleasure" (2 Pet. 2:13); "some count slackness" (2 Pet. 3:9); and Christians are "to count" the delay of the Lord's coming salvation (2 Pet. 3:15). In this meaning of the mental process, Christians are "to esteem" (*hēgeisthai*) whose who labor among them (1 Thess. 5:13).

In a participial form, *hēgeisthai* denotes the status of the Messiah (Matt. 2:6); the leader among the disciples who is to be as one who serves (Luke 22:26); Joseph's position over Egypt (Acts 7:10); Paul's position as speaker in relation to Barnabas (Acts 14:12); and then Judas and Silas as leading men among the brethren in Jerusalem (Acts 15:22).

It is in this participial form that *hēgeisthai* has a relevance to the topic of elders. The "leaders" *(hēgemenous)* who spake the Word of God are to be remembered and their faith is to be imitated (Heb. 13:7). They are to be obeyed (Heb. 13:17). Verse 24 distinguished between "the leaders" *(hēgemenous)* and the saints *(hagoi)*. Though the N.T. is not explicit in these verses, it is possible that these leaders were "elders."

The related words for ruling: *Hēgemoneuein* ("be leader": Luke 2:2; 3:1); *hēgemonia* ("governorship": Luke 3:1); and *hēgemon* ("governor"; Matt. 2:6; 10:18; Mark 13:9; Luke 21:12; 27:2, 11, 14, 15, 21, 27; 28:14; Luke 20:20; Acts 23:24, 26, 33; 24:1, 10; 26:30; 1 Pet. 2:14) are used for civil rulers but are never used for church leaders in the New Testament. Neither is the church leader ever called an *archōn* (ruler, lord, prince) or *depotēs* (master), nor is he said to have *exousia* ("authority") or *dunamis* ("power").

Nevertheless, from the general association of *hēgeisthai* with ruling, one is tempted to conclude that here at last we have indisputable authority for a ruling concept in connection with the leadership of the church. However, before one makes up his mind in which of these varieties of meanings he will understand the uses of *hēgeisthai* in Hebrews 13:7, 17, 24, there are some questions he needs to ask. Did Paul have ruling authority over Barnabas when he was the "chief speaker" *(ho hēgoumenos tou logou)* of the pair (Acts 14:12)? Furthermore, what is the position of Judas Barsabbas and Silas in the church of Jerusalem when they are "leading men among the brethren" *(andras hēgoumenos en tois adelphois)* (Acts 15:22)? Does this designation mean they ruled over the brethren; or does it mean that they were outstanding men in the fellowship? What is to be made of, "But you are not like that. Instead the greatest among you should be like the youngest, and the one who

33

rules (*ho hēgoumenos*) as the one who serves (*ho diakanōn*; Luke 22:26)?"

CONCLUSION

From this extended survey, it would seem that all the Greek terms when considered from the viewpoint of how the elder should conceive of himself stress images of sacrifice and service rather than images of authority. The elder is God's steward; he is one who serves—he is the servant of the church; he is "the slave (*doulos*) of all" (Mark 10:44); he teaches; he watches in behalf of souls; he is one who cares for the church of God; he admonishes and he pleads. He is not a lord over God's heritage (the verb in 1 Pet. 5:3 is the same as that used in Mark 10:42ff.); he is an example (1 Pet. 5:3).

From the viewpoint of the people, the elder is an example to be followed; a teacher from whom to learn; a shepherd whose voice one heeds; a protector from wolves; a leader to whom one submits in humility because he is God's steward; and an older man to whom due respect is gladly given.

If one may state what appears a paradox, the elder should conceive of himself, not in terms of authority, but in terms of doing "a good work"; while the congregation should relate to him as to God's steward. The recalcitrant may be reminded that Paul admonished the Corinthians:

> You know that the household of Stephanas were the first converts in Achaia, and they have devoted themselves to the service of the saints; I urge you to be subject to such men and to every fellow worker and laborer (1 Cor. 16:15, 16).

NOTES

[1]Mishna, *Berakoth* 5:5.

[2]1 Clement 44:5; 47:6; 54:2; 57:1; Polycarp 5:3.

[3]J. W. McGarvey, *The Eldership* (Murfreesboro, Tenn.: Dehoff Publications, 1950; reprint of 1870 edition), p. 9.

[4]F. J. A. Hort, *The Christian Ecclesia* (London: Macmillan, 1914), p. 196.

[5]Law #71; trans. in J. B. Pritchard, ed., *Ancient Near Eastern Texts Related to the Old Testament* (Princeton: Princeton Univ. Press, 1969),

p. 92. R. de Vaux, *Ancient Israel*, trans. by John McHugh (New York: McGraw-Hill Book Co., 1961), p. 118.

[6]R. de Vaux, *op. cit.*, p. 118.

[7]W. H. Bennett, "Elders (Semitic)" in *Hastings' Encyclopaedia of Religion and Ethics*, V, 254.

[8]E. Schürer, *The Jewish People in the Time of Jesus Christ*, trans. by Sophia Taylor and Peter Christie (Edinburgh: T. & T. Clark, 1885), II. 1. 165f.

[9]Trans. in R. K. Harrison, *Archaeology of the New Testament* (London: The English Universities Press, 1964), p. 5.

[10]A. E. Harvey, "Elders," *Journal of Theological Studies*, N.S., 25 (1974): 325-26.

[11]A. Deissmann, *Bible Studies*, trans. by A. Grieve (Edinburgh: T. & T. Clark, 1901), p. 154-56.

[12]Jack P. Lewis, "Authority?" *Harding Graduate School of Religion Bulletin* 18 (June, 1978): 1, 2.

[13]H. W. Beyer, "*Episkopos,*" in *Theological Dictionary of the New Testament*, ed. G. Kittel, trans. by G. W. Bromiley (Grand Rapids, Mich.: W. B. Eerdmans, 1965), II, 608-22.

[14]Ibid., II, 608.

[15]J. W. McGarvey, *op. cit.*, p. 17.

[16]Bruce M. Metzger, ed., *A Textual Commentary on the Greek New Testament* (London/New York: United Bible Societies, 1971), pp. 695, 696.

[17]H. W. Beyer, *op. cit.*, II, 610, 612.

[18]Ibid., II, 616, 617.

[19]Letter #288, trans. in D. W. Thomas, ed., *Documents From Old Testament Times* (Edinburgh and London: Thomas Nelson and Sons, 1958; New York: Harper & Bros., 1961), p. 43.

[20]Trans. in D. W. Thomas, *op. cit.*, p. 51; see also J. Jeremias, "*Poimnē*" in Kittel, *op. cit.*, VI, 486, 487.

[21]B. Reicke, "*Proistemē*" in Kittel, *op. cit.*, VI, 700-703.

[22]Ibid., VI, 702.

[23]F. J. A. Hort, *op. cit.*, p. 127.

[24]B. Reicke, *op. cit.*, VI, 702.

[25]Ibid.

5

Elders—Lords Over God's Heritage?

The Lord provided for elders in every congregation, instructing them to feed his flock by teaching and by example while safeguarding them against grievous wolves (Acts 20:28ff.). Elders are to exercise the oversight willingly, not of constraint (1 Pet. 5:2). They can only do that in keeping with their understanding of God's word and of what is best for God's people.

Members of the Lord's church are to submit to the elders (Heb. 13:17), regarding them highly in love for their work's sake. They are to obey them for they watch in behalf of our souls (1 Tim. 5:17). I have never been able to grasp the logic of those people who select a group of men to be their leaders and who then fault every decision those men make. The most valuable thing about a man is his power of judgment. If a man's judgment has been demonstrated to be poor, he should not be made an elder. I do not think it is right in matters of opinion for people to rise in revolt against the elders. Creating tension between the elders and the congregation is one of the most effective devices of the devil.

Though we are to submit to the elders, they, like the prophets of old (Deut. 13:1ff.), are not at liberty to seduce the Lord's people into error. While a charge against an elder must be based on adequate evidence—at the mouth of two or three witnesses (1 Tim. 5:19)—the elder is not completely exempt from being accused of error. He can fall into reproach and the snare of the devil (1 Tim. 3:6, ASV). The duty of obedience to the elders is not an absolute one, but holds only when elders lead in right things and in right ways. We must obey God and not men (Acts 5:29). Elders cannot authorize what God has forbidden; they cannot prohibit what he has permitted or has commanded. To do so would be to tempt God (Acts 15:10). Though there may have been times when I would have preferred a different decision from the one made, I personally, over the course of a lifetime in the church, do not recall a single instance in which I had to make a decision between obeying God and obeying the elders. The elders I have known—though not all equally qualified—have been godly men who were sincerely trying to serve the Lord.

The question of whether the congregation should revolt is an entirely different question from that of what submission the elders should expect and demand in matters of opinion. A large majority of the questions that elders have to deal with are not matters of right and wrong in the sense of being for or against specific teaching of God's Word. They involve elements of judgment. Elders decide what Bible school literature is to be used; what song book is to be used; what the budget is to be; what kind of buildings are to be provided; how they are to be lighted; what the order of the worship service is to be; what hours the congregation is to meet; who is to do the preaching, the teaching, and song leading; whether men should wear coats and ties at the Lord's table; whether latecomers should wait until the end of the song to enter the auditorium; who is to serve on the various committees; who is to be supported in the mission field and how much.

Ordinarily a preacher's service with a congregation is not terminated because he is teaching error. It merely becomes a matter of opinion that the well-being of the congregation would be served by the preacher's moving on. What elders can peaceably do in all these areas and other like areas depends on the confidence their people have in them. Wise elders should not needlessly defy the wishes of their people. A man can be a leader only when he has followers. People cannot be made to do things. They voluntarily submit to the leadership of a group of elders, and when they are no longer willing to follow, they (in fact, if not in right) move on to another congregation whose elders they are more willing to follow.

In the modern world with its mobility of people an elder may be leading people who on many Biblical questions are better trained than he and who in general are better informed than he. A man is not necessarily chosen because of his superior knowledge. We have developed a system in which our preachers are ordinarily better trained than are our elders. A preacher may teach a man the truth, watch him grow in the Christian life and become an elder, and then may become subject to him when the preacher has had far more experience in the Christian life and knows far more about God's Word than does the elder. Shall the elder expect his will to be dominant over others in all matters of opinion?

A trait of disposition to be cultivated by all Christians is that they are to be "open to reason" (James 3:17). However, in actuality, not all men—not even all elders—are by disposition open to reason. Yet in the Lord's order an elder is subject to admonition by those whom he leads: "Rebuke not an elder, but admonish him as a father" (1 Tim. 5:11). One would assume that the Biblical threat, "He who is often reproved yet stiffens his neck will suddenly be broken beyond healing" (Prov. 29:1), also applies to elders.

Some years back elders in some congregations withdrew from those ladies who shortened their hair (now all ladies do it and none would dare criticize); in some they withdrew from those who attended the movies (but that was before we all got televisions in our living rooms). I recently heard of a group of elders who ruled that only ladies who had arthritis could wear pantsuits to the services. It would be interesting to see how they are going to enforce their decision. Elders known to me decided that a young black boy could not lead singing in a worship service the young people were conducting merely because he was black. Though there are certain essential matters on which we all agree, we are not a people of one faith and practice everywhere believed and practiced in the same way. There are variations in practices from congregation to congregation even in the same geographical area. What is acceptable in one area may be quite out of vogue in another.

Alexander Campbell, Jacob Creath, Jr., Robert Milligan, Moses E. Lard, and J. W. McGarvey criticized certain renderings in the King James Version and advocated the need of Bible revision. H. T. Anderson published his Bible translation in 1864. David Lipscomb said that the ASV was a more accurate translation than the KJV. These men attempted to persuade others of their conclusions, but they did not attempt to decree that others must accept them.

The question of ruling in matters of opinion is particularly pertinent at this time when we are confronted with the Bible version question. Today one group of elders rules that only the King James Version can be read in the services and teaching programs of their congregation; another rules that the KJV and the ASV (which differs from the KJV in 36,000 instances in the New Testament) are the only ones to be read; a third rules that it may be the KJV, ASV, and RSV; a fourth that the NASV and/or NIV may also be included; while still others may have no ruling at all. A person who moves about may find himself in good standing in one congregation but then frowned upon in another because of his reading preferences. None would question the right of a publishing house to say that all material it publishes will use a particular version. What it publishes is its business. Those who agree with the preference will buy the literature and those who do not can go elsewhere.

Can elders rule for the use of a particular version in the public service of their congregation? Certainly they can just as they can decide on a thousand other matters of opinion; but whether or not they will be followed depends on whether their decision corresponds with what most of their people are willing to do. Whether or not they *can* rule is an entirely different question from that of whether or not they *should*. J. W. McGarvey said, "No man can afford any longer to be dependent on the old English version," and also said,

> The Canterbury revision of the New Testament should now totally supplant the King James Version, not only because it is a great improvement as a version, but because it is the only representative in English of the corrected Greek text ("Preacher's Methods," *Missouri Christian Lectures*, 1883, p. 93).

When men rule that people must study the KJV they are binding them to that which is a less reliable representative of God's Word than they otherwise could have. Their act may be that of zeal which is not enlightened.

Will elders accomplish more by ordering their people, or will they accomplish more by teaching their people? Instances could be found where men have ruled and expected to be followed on questions on which they have not spent five minutes teaching. Instances can be found where they have ruled on questions on which they would not be capable of teaching. People who could not translate one verse if their life depended on it often have fixed ideas about what is good and bad in translation—ideas usually dependent on previous exposure. They prefer to maintain the status quo. Across history in religious matters a sizable group of people have always preferred the old, even when it was defective, to the new. There has been significant opposition to every important translation that has appeared.

This whole topic raises a larger question. Did the Lord provide for the rule of his church by teaching and example, or did he provide for leadership by decree? Personally, I am afraid that those least capable to teach are the most ready to decree what they cannot teach. As I would see it, if one cannot persuade people of what is right and what is wrong—of what is good and evil—by teaching and admonition, one is not likely to be successful with force.

6

A Self-Perpetuating Board?

In the congregation in which I grew up there was a plurality of elders as the Scriptures teach there should be in every congregation. I think, however, that no one who knew the congregation at that time would want to deny that in this plurality there was a leading elder. Two of the elders had special chairs in which they sat for their own comfort during the services, rather than on the pews, giving them an obvious position of respect. Among some denominationalists in the community, the congregation was spoken of as "Tom Brown's [fictitious name] church." When the time came that this good brother, who was highly respected by all, was faced with the incapacities of advancing age, he appointed his successor to the position of elder.

The appointee, though a good man, was quite dogmatic and did not have the "followership" in the congregation that a leader has to have. One cannot lead if there are no followers. Something of the goodness of the appointee came out (in my opinion) in that he realized in a short time that his position was impossible. Though the atmosphere of the time was one of debating whether one once an elder was always an elder and one that had coined a rural proverbial expression "A mule can as well resign his muleship as an elder can resign his eldership," he saw it otherwise. Without undue pressure from others, the brother voluntarily terminated his appointment, remained in the congregation, and continued teaching his Bible class as he had done for years before. There is much work in the vineyard apart from being an elder!

Let us use this episode as a takeoff point to raise the question if the eldership is really a self-perpetuating board. Since Scripture gives so little on the question of how men are made elders, the question has largely to be answered on the basis of judgment. Paul and Barnabas appointed elders in the congregations established on the first missionary journey (Acts 14:23). Titus was left by Paul in Crete to appoint elders in every church (Tit. 1:5). If we have other specific cases, they have escaped my notice. There were elders in Jerusalem (Acts 11:30; 15:2), Ephesus (Acts 20:17), and Philippi (Phil. 1:1); but how they were selected and appointed is not revealed. Those in Ephesus had been made overseers by the Holy Spirit (Acts 20:28), but who can say what methods the Spirit used to make the choice known? Qualifications are given in 1 Timothy 3 and Titus 1, and attitudes to be manifested toward elders by people in the congregations are given in 1 Timothy 1:5, 17. Some of these attitudes are to be manifested toward any older man; but where does the initiative lie in making men to be elders different from other older men in the congregation?

At an earlier stage of our movement, the preachers often were the tool through which the congregation expressed its will; and there may still be cases where this system prevails. There usually was not an abundance of candidates. The population was more stable than it is now. People were born and died in one community. Their lives were known to all. At the time of the summer meeting the preacher announced that such and such brothers would be considered candidates; and if no objection was voiced, before the meeting was out, announced that they had been appointed. The case of Titus's appointing elders in Crete was thought to furnish a Biblical precedent. The success of the system was dependent on to what extent the visiting preacher's initiative really gave action to the will of the congregation. Who can deny that in many cases it worked well?

The shortcomings of the system can be seen in the danger that the preachers run the congregations by the appointments they make. It can also be seen in two specific illustrations. In the one, a preacher came by and appointed some men to be elders. Later when problems developed in the congregation over leadership, no one seemed even to remember the preacher's name who had created the situation. Without going into the details of the other demonstrations of lack of qualifications on the part of the appointees, one can say that one man of them finally left his wife, telling her that if he wanted a different woman every night, he would have her.

In the second illustration, the preacher arrived for a Sunday appointment at a congregation he knew nothing about. He was told by the elder who was in his nineties that the congregation was selecting a new elder and that "Brother . . ." was the candidate. The preacher was supposed to make him an elder. All the preacher could do was to say that he had been asked to officiate—that if "Brother . . ." was indeed qualified and was the choice of the congregation, from there on, they should consider him an elder. On the other hand, if "Brother . . ." was not qualified [the preacher had never heard of him before], then "Brother . . ." as a Christian should, himself, decline the appointment. It served the preacher right when within two years, after he had preached on the qualifications of elders on an occasion that the "Brother . . ." had announced another candidate for the eldership, he was fired on the spot.

In large city congregations, the elders usually select the persons who are to be considered for elders. They may allow the congregation to submit names, and in some cases only those who get the most votes will be seriously considered. After all, democracy is the American form of government, even if it is not the Biblical one!

One can defend the system by noting that it assures that some people will be willing to follow. He can also defend it by asking who in the congregation is in the best position to know who is qualified to be an elder? All things being equal, the elders should be. But all

45

things are not always equal. Elders do not always know the people in their congregations. Big congregations are big business, and in cases where elders have been chosen because they are aggressive business men, they are not always its best informed men on the Scriptures; they are not always its best teachers; they are not always its most spiritual men. However, they convince themselves that they must safeguard the flock, they want to work with congenial men, so the board perpetuates the board in its own image.

Against this system of perpetuation is the problem of the "in crowd" versus the "out crowd." We are blind if we try to convince ourselves that politics do not affect the eldership. With the present elders responsible for saying when new candidates can be considered and with their screening all the candidates, the only way a congregation can change its direction (such as when it has outgrown the vision of its elders) has to take on the appearance of a revolt against its leadership.

I once preached briefly for a congregation in which an elder appointed his brother to be an elder. More than half the congregation walked out, joined neighboring congregations and began an active campaign to dissuade any new people from fellowship in the congregation they had left. The remaining "out crowd" shortly came to the device of withholding all contributions, and most participation, in order to break the hold of the "in crowd." Eventually, when the congregation was on the verge of losing its property, the "out crowd" and the "in crowd" secured temporary aid from a sister congregation on the condition that the "in crowd" would resign and leave the congregation. Without question, they should have. One of them eventually did time in the penitentiary, though not because of a church related offense. But glad to be relieved from the bear they had by the tail, the "in crowd" accepted the conditions. In a short time the "out crowd," who had not even been faithful in attendance during the strife, secured appointments for themselves and became the new "in crowd." Christian? Well, you say!

Yet another problem of the system is the "closed corporation" problem. The board has its quota of members. Other men who may have reasonable qualifications are not in line for consideration for one reason or another—whether it is that they are not "in" with the earlier appointees or are not well-known to them. In any city of size you can see these men moving to new congregations, opportunities opening to them, and their being appointed elders in a relatively short time—an opportunity to serve that never would have been theirs in the "closed corporation." Also in our cities one can sometimes sense that one of the stimuli for starting a new congregation is the offering of an opportunity for men to move into leadership positions who would not soon have that opportunity if they remained with the older congregation.

I recently heard of a case of a man, once a preacher, who was suggested by some in his congregation as a candidate for being an elder; but he was refused by the existing elders because they thought he knew so much more about the Bible than they did that they would have difficulty in working with him.

I have never had any question about the Lord's provision for elders in every congregation. Nor have I questioned that they are to be highly regarded in love for their work's sake. That the Lord had in mind a board, I highly question; and that it was to be a self-perpetuating one, all the more so!

Only small deviations make the difference between genuine dollars and counterfeit ones; were it not so, no one would be deceived by them. Every aspect of the Christian life has its slight deviation which makes it look like the Lord's plan, but yet is different from it. The appeal of power and prestige continuously seduces all people. Example of life and influence for good that comes through understanding the Word and living with the Lord in sacrificial service are more difficult to maintain. The good shepherd lays down his life for the sheep.

There is no easy solution known to me for the problem I have raised. If we had thoroughly qualified men, it really would not matter how they are appointed. It is easy for dominant people to impose their will on a congregation in the appointment of its elders. With the problem of caring for widows, the apostles did not do that. They said to the Grecians, "You select men of good repute, full of

47

the Spirit and of wisdom" (Acts 6:3). Today we would likely say of that procedure, "It may give us 'soreheads' who will be hard to work with."

It is all too easy to engage in open fault-finding with men who are discharging what proves to be a thankless task. At the same time, it can hardly be denied that while hours are spent in weekly meetings taking care of necessary business, the words of Ezekiel indict our efforts:

> The weak you have not strengthened, the sick you have not healed, the crippled you have not bound up, the strayed you have not brought back, the lost you have not sought. . . . My sheep were scattered, they wandered over all the mountains and on every high hill; my sheep were scattered over all the face of the earth, with none to search or seek for them (Ezek. 34:4, 6).

7

Greek Word Studies on the Function and Authority of Preachers

The modern preacher who devotes his energies to church administration, to counseling, and to preaching sermons to people, most of whom have already obeyed the Gospel, has no close parallel in the church of the first century. He is a hybrid personality that has evolved out of some elements that go back to the New Testament itself, out of our contact with our religious neighbors, out of the failure of our elders to find time and skill to shepherd the flock, out of a recognized necessity to deal with the needs of straying people, out of the need of our people to have their ears tickled regularly, and out of the specialization of our times. As the preacher becomes more prominent—the executive, the most influential figure of our congregations—the elders become the board of directors, but with less clearly defined status. In far too many cases the preacher dominates the elders rather than being subordinate to them. In far too many cases they are being led by him and are only rubber stamping his plans rather than furnishing leadership. Our task is to look at certain Greek words which may suggest what the position and work of the preacher were in the New Testament.

I. WORDS FOR THE PREACHER AS A CHRISTIAN

A. Doulos

There are certain Greek words describing the preacher which also describe every Christian. These words are very significant in determining how the preacher should conceive of himself. The first of these is *doulos* ("slave"). The N.T. has a series of words in the "serving" category. They include *diakanos* ("minister"; John 2:5; Matt. 22:12; etc.), *misthōtos* (Mark 1:20; John 10:12) or *misthios* (the "hired servant"; Luke 15:19); *therapōn* ("servant," or "attendant"; Heb. 3:5); and *pais* ("boy" or "slave"; Matt. 8:6, 13; 14:2; Luke 15:26). However, it is the word *doulos* ("slave") which is the most common word.

The *doulos* (the Greek equivalent of *'ebed* in the O.T.) is the man bought in the marketplace so that he is not his own. His function is to do the will of another. The centurion said, "I say to my slave, do this, and he does it" (Matt. 8:9). In Jesus' parable of the plowing slave (Luke 17:7-10) the rhetorical question is "Will he [the owner] thank the slave because he did what was commanded?" The slave was bought to work, and he deserves no thanks for doing it. In the N.T., along with this word *doulos* is a variant form, *sundoulos* ("fellow slave"; Matt. 18:28, 29, 31, 33; 24:49; Col. 1:7; 4:7; Rev. 6:11; 19:10; 22:9) whose basic meaning is not different. Our English versions in general have weakened for the English reader the force of these words by rendering them "servant," "bond-servant," and "fellow-servant." With these English renderings we are more likely to think of an employee than to think of a slave.

New Testament writers repeatedly speak of themselves as "slaves of God" or "of Christ": "Paul, a slave of Jesus Christ" (Rom. 1:1); "Simon Peter, a slave and apostle of Jesus Christ" (2 Pet. 1:1); "Jude, a slave of Jesus Christ" (Jude 1); and "James, a slave of God and the Lord Jesus Christ" (James 1:1).

Everyone is a slave to someone—if to no other, then to the most galling of masters—to his own passions. "Everyone who commits sin is a slave to sin" (John 8:34). We changed masters when we became Christians. Paul informs us that we were slaves of sin, but have become slaves of righteousness (Rom. 6:17). We are to "Live as free men, yet without using your freedom as a pretext for evil; but live as slaves of God" (1 Pet. 2:16).

A whole medley of ideas centers around the idea of the preacher's being a slave. As the slave of God, it is his task to heed the voice of God, not the voice of the people. "Or am I trying to please men? If I were still pleasing men, I should not be a slave of Christ" (Gal. 1:10). "Who are you to pass judgment on the slave of another? It is before his own master that he stands or falls" (Rom. 14:4). Of John Knox it was said that his fear of God was so great that he did not fear any man.[1] In moments of truth, all we who preach the Word must confess, at least to ourselves, that we have felt the impulse which made the prophets of the O.T. (whom we designate "false prophets") proclaim what the people wanted to hear. We have been tempted to say, "Thus saith the Lord" over that which the Lord has not spoken.

But the preacher is not only the slave of the Lord, he is also the slave of his people; however, here is a different aspect of the slave relation from that of obedience. This time it is humble service. Jesus in coming to earth took the form of a slave (Phil. 2:7). It is in view of his own slave relationship that Paul declared, "Though I am free from all men, I have made myself a slave to all that I might win the more" (1 Cor. 9:19). Again he declares, "For what we preach is not ourselves, but Jesus Christ as Lord, with ourselves as your slaves for Jesus' sake" (2 Cor. 4:5).

One well-known preacher has stated as his rule of life that if anyone asks him to do something, he tries to do it if he can at all. He is slave to his people. But in contrast with that attitude, in certain cases which have come to my attention across the years, preachers have said to their people, "I will come preach for you if you put wall-to-wall carpet in the preacher's home"; "I will work for you if you increase the salary"; "I will work with you if you furnish such and such fringe benefits." The availability of prestige pulpits and high salaries can easily convince one that he has had a call to greater service.

It is not possible for my mind to conceive that the apostle Paul, or any N.T. figure, would have gauged his service by any such yardsticks. With apologies to John F. Kennedy, the late President of the United States, the concept of preacher as slave should be stated, "Do not ask what your people can do for you, but what you can do for your people!" Like his Lord, the preacher is not to be ministered unto, but is to minister (Mark 10:45). Jesus talked about a greatness that one attained, not by exercising authority as rulers of the world do, but by being a *diakanos* ("servant") and a *doulos* ("slave"; Matt. 20:26, 27).

B. Oikonomos

A second interesting word used for the preacher and also used for every Christian is *oikonomos*; which is *ben-bayith* in Hebrew; and means "steward." The term assumes the use of the figure of speech of the "household" for the kingdom. The church is the "household of God" (1 Tim. 3:15). Fourteen passages in the KJV have the word "steward" (singular: Gen. 15:2; 43:19; 1 Kings 16:9; Luke 12:42; 16:1, 3, 8; Tit. 1:7; plural: 1 Chron. 28:1; 1 Cor. 4:1, 2; 1 Pet. 4:10), ordinarily designating secular relationships, but in a few cases spiritual ones. Two of the cases (Matt. 20:8; Luke 8:3) render *epitropos*—a word with which we are not concerned here.

The related noun *oikonomia* means "stewardship" and is so rendered three times in the KJV in the Parable of the Unjust Steward (Luke 16:2, 3, 4). However, in one of those unexplainable inconsistencies of translation, the KJV under the influence of the Latin version rendered *oikonomia* as "dispensation" in four passages (1 Cor. 9:17; Eph. 1:10; 3:2; Col. 1:25). "Assignment" would be a better choice.[2] The preacher has an "assignment" to complete (1 Tim. 1:4).

The "steward" is the man who has been entrusted with the business of another, and the discharging of that function is his "stewardship." This relationship is seen in the parable of the wise steward set over the household (Luke 12:42; cf. Matt. 24:45 where *doulos* is used) and in the unjust steward of Jesus' parable (Luke 16:1, 2). The minor heir is under guardians *(epitropoi)* and stew-

52

ards (*oikonomoi*; Gal. 4:1, 2). These two terms are to be regarded as synonymous. They reproduce the *(paidagōgus)* metaphor used in Gal. 3:24, 25.

Every Christian is called upon to serve.

> As each has received a gift, employ it for one another as good stewards of God's varied grace: Whoever speaks, as one who utters oracles of God; whoever renders service, as one who renders it by the strength God supplies; in order that in everything God may be glorified through Jesus Christ (1 Pet. 4:10, 11).

The bishop also is a steward and as God's "steward" must be blameless (Tit. 1:7).

The special type of stewardship of the preacher is a stewardship of the Word. Paul speaks of himself and his associates: "This is how one should regard us, as servants of Christ and stewards of the mysteries of God. Moreover it is required of stewards that they be found faithful" ([*pistos*, cf. Luke 16:10] 1 Cor. 4:1, 2). The steward has been entrusted with a teaching that he has no right to modify, for which he must give a strict account unto his master.[3]

C. Didaskalos

A third word is *didaskalos* ("teacher"). Teachers were among those having spiritual gifts in the N.T. church (Rom. 12:7; 1 Cor. 12:28; Eph. 4:11); but, that every Christian should also aim at this service is expounded in the admonition, "For though by this time you ought to be teachers, you need someone to teach you again the first principles of God's word" (Heb. 5:12). The Christian woman is to teach what is good (Tit. 2:3). The elder is to be a skilled teacher (*didaktikos*; 1 Tim. 3:2).

The grandeur of the teacher can be seen in the fact that, though described as both teaching and preaching (Matt. 4:23; 9:35), Jesus is more often described in the Gospels in the role of teacher—whether one thinks of the use of *didaskalos*, *rabbi*, or *hypistos*—than he is in the role of a preacher (cf. Jn. 3:2). He taught "as one who had authority" (Matt. 7:28, 29). The Sermon on the Mount was "teaching," not "preaching."

Teaching in the work of preaching is seen in the presence of the prophets and teachers in Antioch (Acts 13:1). Paul, in addition to being a preacher and an apostle, was appointed as a teacher (2 Tim. 1:11), and he issued admonitions to teaching in the Epistles to Timothy and Titus: "Command and teach these things" (1 Tim. 4:11). "Till I come, attend to the public reading of Scripture, to preaching, to teaching" (1 Tim. 4:13). "And what you have heard from me before many witnesses, entrust to faithful men who will be able to teach others also" (2 Tim. 2:2). Timothy is able to teach (2 Tim. 2:24; *didaktikos*); and Titus to "Teach what befits with sound doctrine" (Tit. 2:1). When the preacher is torn between the poles of making the thrust of his preaching to be teaching or motivation, he would do well to consider the import of *didaskalos*.

D. Ergatēs
A fourth word to consider is *ergatēs*. The preacher is "a workman *(ergatēs)* who has no need to be ashamed, rightly handling the word of truth" (2 Tim. 2:15). Jesus said that the harvest is plentiful, but the workmen are few (Matt. 9:37, 38; Luke 10:2). The workman is worthy of his food (or wages) (Matt. 10:10; Luke 10:7; 1 Tim. 5:18). The basic significance of this descriptive term can be seen in the parable in which workmen are hired at various hours to work in the vineyard (Matt. 20:1-16) and in the denunciation of the rich in the Epistle of James who are accused of withholding the wages of the workmen (James 5:4). *Ergatēs* also designates the workmen of Ephesus (Acts 19:25) who participated in the riot.

The idea of the preacher as a workman suggests the need to put in an honest day's work and an honest week's work. It is the opposite of the sluggard who is holding a sinecure. The preacher is to be diligent (2 Tim. 2:15).

The numerous places in the N.T. in which the activities of the Christian are described in terms of the verb *ergazesthai* and of the companion noun *ergon* ("work") should not be obliterated in a theological clash over the relative value of faith and works. The Lord redeemed us from all iniquity "to purify for himself people of his own who are zealous for good works" (Tit. 2:14). Those who aid traveling persons are "fellow workers in the truth" (3 John 8).

The converse of the good workman concept is to be seen in those passages where Paul admonishes Christians to beware of "evil-workers" (Phil. 3:2) and charges that some are "false apostles, deceitful workmen" (2 Cor. 11:13). Finally, at the Judgment the Lord will say to some, "Depart from me all you workers of iniquity" (Luke 13:27).

Timothy is Paul's fellow worker (*sunergos*; Rom. 16:21) as well as being God's fellow worker (1 Thess. 3:2; cf. 1 Cor. 3:9). A whole host of other people, including Titus (2 Cor. 8:23) and Epaphroditus (Phil. 2:25) are said to be Paul's fellow workers (Rom. 16:3, 9; 2 Cor. 1:24; Phil. 4:3; Col. 4:11; Philem. 1:24).

II. THE DISTINCTIVE WORK OF THE PREACHER

A. Kērux

The first of the Greek words unique for the preacher's work is *kērux* ("the herald"). The O.T. equivalent of *kērux* is *karoz* (Dan. 3:4) which is a Greek loan word in Hebrew also meaning "herald." The term *kērux*, itself, occurs also in the Septuagint at Genesis 41:43; Ecclesiasticus 20:15; 4 Maccabees 6:4, and is the term from which our word "preacher" derives. The *kērux* is the individual who announces *(kērussein)* a message that is not his own. It was the message and not the herald, himself, who was important. The herald was the mouthpiece of the one who had sent him. He did not take up his audience's time trying to appear clever. Absolute fidelity to his message was required of him. His message had the authority of the one who had sent him.

The term *kērux* occurs three times in the N.T. Noah was a preacher of righteousness (2 Pet. 2:5). Then Paul twice declares that he was appointed a herald and an apostle (1 Tim. 2:7; 2 Tim. 1:11). In the O.T., the prophets had acted in a similar capacity though the term *karoz* (or *kērux*) is not specifically applied to them. The verb *qara'* (translated in some O.T. settings by *kērussein*) is used in a host of passages in Jeremiah for preaching activity (2:2; 4:5; 7:2; 11:16; 19:2; 20:8; cf. Is. 40:6; 44:7; 58:1). Ezekiel pointed out that such a person is like a watchman set on the wall who sees the danger approaching and who must sound the alarm or be guilty of the death of those in the city (Ezek. 3:16ff.; 33:1ff.). The prophets' fixed introductory phrase was "Thus says the Lord."

In the N.T., faith comes by hearing; hearing comes through preaching (Rom. 10:17); and men preach who are sent (Rom. 10:15) from God (2 Cor. 5:18). The preachers were not those who informed the people of their personal opinions on a number of topics. They were not those who devoted time narrating a wealth of trivia. To the contrary Paul said: "For what we preach is not ourselves, but Jesus Christ as Lord, with ourselves as your slaves for Jesus' sake" (2 Cor. 4:5). We all have much trouble in distinguishing our opinions from the Gospel we are to preach. Often in our preaching we are doing no more than informing people of what we think on this and that. But what difference does it make what opinions one holds? Of what significance is his position to anyone except himself? Is he setting himself up as the measuring stick of right and wrong? Is he, as it were, issuing papal decrees on various topics? The message the *kērux* has been sent to announce is the significant thing; his opinions are nothing. We preachers need to remember that we must give the lost person God's Word, not ours. God has promised to bless his Word, not ours; and it was his Word, not ours, that will not return void.

We have a captive audience and we can consume their time with the detail of our week's activities, with where we have been, with our family conditions, and with our private interests—all of which have relevance only to ourselves. Certainly all Christians should be concerned with the joys, the sorrows, and the well-being of all other Christians—including the preacher and his family—but have you thought of the fact that we know relatively little about Paul's life and of his family? We do know the Word he preached!

As Paul saw it, even the motives that prompted the preaching were of less significance than was the fact that Christ was being preached (Phil. 1:15-18). The messenger's life might contradict that which he announced (1 Cor. 9:27; 2 Tim. 2:1-7; 4:5); and in such a case, the messenger of unworthy life, after preaching, might himself be lost. The herald is to preach when the times seem favorable and when they seem unfavorable (2 Tim. 4:2). To receive the herald is to receive the one who sent him, and to reject him is to reject the one who sent him (Matt. 10:40).

Kērugma, a noun also derived from the root *kērussein*, means "preaching." It occurs in the Septuagint as the translation for both *Qol* and *Qeri'ah*. It is in the N.T. eight times for the act of preaching, referring to the preaching of Jonah (Matt. 12:41; Luke 11:32) and to Gospel preaching by Paul and others (Rom. 16:25; 1 Cor. 1:21; 2:4; 15:14; 2 Tim. 4:17; Tit. 1:3). It does not occur in the N.T. in the sense made popular in modern theology by C. H. Dodd,[5] namely, to describe the basic content of the message of the early Christian preaching.

B. Euangelistēs

Euangelistēs ("evangelist") occurs three times in the N.T.: once describing Philip (Acts 21:28); once describing one of the gifts listed in Ephesians (Eph. 4:11); and once describing the work Timothy is charged to do (2 Tim. 4:5). The term "evangelist" describes a function one discharges, not an office he holds.[6] While all the apostles were evangelists, not all evangelists were apostles. The task of the evangelist was to "preach the word" (2 Tim. 4:2). In post-apostolic church history the evangelists came to be considered the successors of the apostles.[7] The term then also takes on the sense of an "author of a Gospel."[8] However, these are post-Biblical developments.[9]

The verb *euangelizesthai* is fifty-five times in the N.T. Its O.T. background is *basar*, "to announce the good news of salvation" (Is. 40:9; 52:7; 61:1; Ps. 96:2). Twenty-three N.T. occurrences of *euangelizesthai* are rendered in the KJV as "preach"; twenty-two as "preach the Gospel"; two as "bring good tidings" (Luke 2:10; 1 Thess. 3:6); two as "show glad tidings" (Luke 1:19; 8:1); once "bring glad tidings" (Rom. 10:15b); once "declare" (Rev. 10:7); once "declare glad tidings" (Acts 13:32); and then there are three (Acts 14:7; Gal. 1:11; 1 Pet. 1:25) miscellaneous renderings. There is also the verb *proeuangelizomai* (Gal. 3:8), "to preach the Gospel in advance." The promise that in Abraham all nations would be blessed is an announcing of good news before the good news became a reality.

Euangelion (the message announced) occurs seventy-seven times. It is most often rendered "Gospel" (46 t.); but also is modified as "Gospel of Christ" (11 t.); "Gospel of God" (7 t.); and "Gospel of the kingdom" (3 t.). By the second century *euangelion* had come to mean the written message of salvation.[10] Then each individual book came to be called a gospel.[11]

The distinction which is standard among us, between the local preacher and the evangelist who travels, is a distinction unknown to the N.T. and one which has come into our thought through denominational influences. The fundamental idea in the N.T. in preaching is the telling of news to people who had not heard it before—what we call evangelization. It has nothing to do with the delivery of sermons to the converted.[12]

C. Katangellein

Another word not greatly different from *kērussein* and *euangelizein* is *katangellein* ("to announce") which occurs in eighteen passages, while its corresponding noun *katangelous* occurs once (Acts 17:18), and is rendered "setter forth" (KJV and NIV) or "preacher" (RSV). In these words the messenger as contrasted with the teacher is stressed.

This verb, *katangellein*, describes the proclamation of the prophets (Acts 3:24) and the proclamation by Jesus of light to the people and to the Gentiles (Acts 26:23). It is frequent for the apostles' proclamation (Acts 4:2, 13:5, 36; 15:36; 16:17, 21; 17:3, 13, 23) of Jesus, of the Word of God, and of the resurrection. The faith of the Romans is proclaimed through the world (Rom. 1:8). The Christian proclaims the Lord's death in the Lord's supper (1 Cor. 11:26); Paul and his company proclaim Christ (1 Cor. 2:1; Col. 1:28). Paul rejoices that though some proclaim Christ out of bad motives, Christ is proclaimed (Phil. 1:17); and finally, those who proclaim the Gospel have a right to live by it (1 Cor. 9:14).[13]

D. Minister

Our use of the word "minister" as a distinguishing designation for the preacher also reflects the penetration of denominational thought and practice into our ranks. In the N.T. there are many persons who minister; but there are not one, two, or five who are "the ministers."

1. Diakanos

Diakanos which lies back of the term "minister" occurs thirty times in the N.T. In the KJV it is twenty times rendered "minister," seven times "servant," and three (where it is in a church organization context) as "deacon" (Phil. 1:1; 1 Tim. 3:8, 12).

As "servant," *diakanos* designates the servants of a king (Matt. 22:13) and the servants in charge of wine at the wedding feast (John 2:5, 9). It occurs in Jesus' statement, "The greatest among you will be your servant" (Matt. 23:11; Mark 9:35); and occurs in the statement "Where I am there shall my servant be also" (John 12:26). Finally, Phoebe is a "servant of the church in Cenchreae" (Rom. 16:1).

This last case is the one time *diakanos* designates a female, and it raises the question whether or not the early church had female appointees. In view of the ambiguity of the term, the passage need mean no more than that Phoebe served the church. The same obscurity resides in the term *gunē* in 1 Timothy 3:11 which can either designate "women" or "wives." If "women," it could give the qualifications of "deaconesses"; but the case is not conclusive. The writer is likely speaking of the wives of the deacons. If we have recourse to history, we learn from Pliny in his letter to Trajan that he has questioned two females—ministers *(ministrae)*—of the church in Bithynia about its practices.[14] This Latin term has the same ambiguity that the two previous Greek terms have and does not demonstrate conclusively that the second century church had female appointees in its organization. Beyond this item, the clear evidence of the second century points to a developing organization of bishops, presbyters and deacons. It is not until one arrives at the third century Church Orders that he finds clear evidence for the deaconesses.[15]

Reverting to consideration of the twenty occurrences of *diakanos* that are rendered "minister" in the KJV, one finds Jesus calling the one who wants to be great to be minister (Matt. 20:26; Mark 10:43); the alternation with "servant" in the next verse is only for English variety; the Greek words are identical. The civil ruler is "God's minister" (Rom. 13:4; *bis*). Christ is the minister of the Jews for the truth of God (Rom. 15:8); Paul and Apollos are ministers through whom the Corinthians have believed (1 Cor. 3:5); the apostles are ministers of a new covenant (2 Cor. 3:6); they are "ministers of God" (2 Cor. 6:4); the devil's ministers appear as ministers of righteousness (2 Cor. 11:15; *bis*); those who oppose Paul claim to be ministers of Christ (2 Cor. 11:23); and Paul asks if Christ is a minister of sin (Gal. 2:17). Then, Paul himself is a minister of the Gospel (Eph. 3:7; Col. 1:23) and a minister to the church in Colossae (Col. 1:25). Tychicus is a faithful minister of the Lord (Eph. 6:21; Col. 4:7); Epaphras is a faithful minister of Christ (Col. 1:7); a manuscript variant (1 Thess. 3:2) calls Timothy "God's minister"; Timothy is called on to be a good minister in Paul's letter to him (1 Tim. 4:6).

The whole emphasis of *diakanos* as used in Paul's writing is on subordination. Paul has very pointed warnings against conceit (Rom. 11:25; 12:16) and has exhortations to submission (1 Cor. 16:16; Heb. 13:17; 1 Pet. 5:5). It becomes obvious that this term has none of the connotations of an authoritarian figure in the congregations.[16] It does not even occur with the definite article— "the minister." It is only a quirk of our English translations that all of the occurrences were not rendered "servant," as some are, instead of "minister."

2. Leitourgos

Another of the words for minister is the *leitourgos* who among the Greeks was one who discharged public office at his own expense. He was a public servant. It is used in five passages of the N.T.: of earthly rulers who discharge functions God has assigned them (Rom. 13:6); of Jesus as minister of the heavenly sanctuary (Heb. 8:2); of angels who are ministering spirits (Heb. 1:7); Ps. 104:4); of Paul as a minister of Christ with the duty to proclaim the Gospel (Rom. 15:16); and finally to Epaphroditus who was sent from Philippi to serve Paul's needs (Phil. 2:25).

The related verb *leitourgein* is three times in the N.T. describing the ministry of prophets and teachers at Antioch (Acts 13:2); the ministry of the Gentile churches to the needs of the poor saints in Jerusalem (Rom. 15:27); and the service of the priests and Levites under the Law (Heb. 10:11; cf. Ex. 29:30; Num. 16:9). The verb has to do with the discharge of a function which is of a representative character.

The adjective *leitourgikos* is once in the phrase "ministering spirits" (Heb. 1:14) describing angels, not men.

The noun *leitourgia* for the discharge of the function of the *leitourgos* is in six passages: for the ministry of Zechariah (Luke 1:23); for the ministry of Jesus when compared with that of the Levitical priests (Heb. 8:6); for the service of the tabernacle (Heb. 9:21); for the ministry of the Corinthian church for the poor of Jerusalem (2 Cor. 9:12); for the offering of the faith of the Philippians (Phil. 2:17); and for what the Philippians could not do for Paul but for which Epaphroditus had almost lost his life (Phil. 2:30).

3. Hupēretēs

A third word for minister is *hupēretēs*. The verb *hupēretein* occurs three times in the N.T. describing the service David rendered his generation (Acts 13:36); the ministering of Paul's hands to his own necessities (Acts 20:34); and the ministering to Paul done by his acquaintances while he was in prison (Acts 24:23).

The noun *hupēretēs* ("minister") occurs twenty-two times and is rendered in the KJV as "officer" eleven times, "minister" five times, and "servant" four times. First, there are those cases where a civil officer is spoken of: the one who executes the decision of the court (Matt. 5:25); those sent by Pharisees and the chief priests to take Jesus early in his ministry (John 7:32, 45, 46); those in the band that come to take Jesus the last night (John 18:3, 12, 18, 22; 19:6); and those who find the apostles absent from the prison and who bring them from the temple to the court (Acts 5:22, 26).

Peter sits with the "servants" in the high priest's palace (Matt. 26:58; Mark 14:54, 65). That the term is rendered "servants," rather than "officers" as in the above cases, is entirely arbitrary. In a final case, Jesus said that were his kingdom of this world, his "servants" would fight (John 18:36).

In addition to these civil usages, there are also religious ones. The one in charge of books at the synagogue is the "minister" (Luke 4:20). Those who have handed on the Gospel messages are "ministers of the word" (Luke 1:2). Mark was the "minister" of Saul and Barnabas (Acts 13:5); and Paul, himself, was made a "minister" and witness by his appointment at the time of his vision on the road to Damascus (Acts 26:16); hence, he calls on the Corinthians to consider him and his co-workers as "ministers of Christ" (1 Cor. 4:1).

In Greek the term *hupēretēs* carries the idea of an under rower on a ship or that of an assistant. The point in common between this word and *oikonomos* ("steward") is this subordinate function and status each implies.

III. GREEK WORDS DESCRIBING THE FUNCTION OF PREACHERS

In addition to the verbs *kērussein* ("to herald"), *legein* ("to speak"), *katangellein* ("to declare," "to announce"), and *didaskein* ("to teach") which we have already considered, there are certain other verbs and nouns—some negative and some positive—describing the work of the preacher which demand our attention. We will look at negative aspects first.

A. Kapēleuein

The verb *kapēleuein* (2 Cor. 2:17) occurs only once in the N.T. and was rendered *adulterare* by the Vulgate. The KJV, influenced by that version, translated the passage: "For we are not as many, which corrupt the word of God. . . . " In its non-biblical usage the word *kapēleuein* has to do with the huckster or small trader in retail trade. Hence there is force in the renderings: ". . . we do not . . . go hawking the word of God about" (NEB); ". . . we do not . . . peddle the word of God" (NASV; NIV); or ". . . we do not handle God's word as though it were cheap merchandise" (TEV). Even the Living Bible Paraphrased gave an apt turn to this passage: "We are not like those hucksters . . . whose idea in getting out the Gospel is to

62

make a good living out of it."

This description of preaching suggests that the showmanship, the double dealing for personal advancement, and the trickery that turn the pulpit into a performance of the sideshow have no place in Gospel preaching.[17]

B. Machesthai

"The slave of God must not strive" (KJV; *ou dei machesthai*, 2 Tim. 2:24; Vulgate; *litigare*). This word occurs only once for the work of the preacher, but occurs for the disputes of the Jews with each other over the teaching of Jesus (John 6:52); for the actual fight of the two Israelites who were rebuked in Egypt by Moses (Ex. 2:13; Acts 7:26), and for the struggle of Christians with each other (James 4:2). Other renderings of the admonition to preachers include "must not quarrel" (NIV); or "must not be quarrelsome" (RSV; NEB; NASV; TEV). The noun corresponding to *machesthai* is *mache* ("fighting") used for struggles Paul encountered in Macedonia (2 Cor. 7:5) and is translated elsewhere as "controversies" (2 Tim. 2:24; Tit. 3:9) and "fightings" (James 4:1).

Granting to start with—as anyone knows who has engaged in a "sensible discussion" with his wife—that some judgment and viewpoint are involved in determining when one has gone beyond "contending earnestly" into quarreling, we certainly have here an area that demands consideration. One hears it said in admiration of a preacher, "he is a fighter." One has sadly observed the clashes between the preacher and his elders, between the preacher and his congregation, and between the preacher and fellow preachers.

C. Ēpios

Turning from the negative traits to more positive ones, we notice that the converse of *machesthai* is *ēpios* ("gentle"; RSV "kindly"; 2 Tim. 2:24). The term describes Paul's behavior toward the Thessalonians when he was among them. "We were gentle among you, like a nurse taking care of children" (1 Thess. 2:7). I am not at all confident that *ēpios* describes the techniques that we preachers have actually used. Furthermore, the preacher is to be "forbearing" (*anexikakos*; 2 Tim. 2:24). This word occurs only once in the N.T.;

but it carries the idea of bearing evil without resentment.[18]

D. Anagnōsis

The preacher is to give himself to reading (*anagnōsis*; Latin: *lectio*; 1 Tim. 4:13). This noun which occurs three times in the N.T. is used for the reading of the law and the prophets in the synagogue (Acts 13:15) and for any reading of the Old Covenant (2 Cor. 3:14). The rabbis put great stress on study of the Torah. Hillel said, "He who does not learn is worthy of death" (Aboth 1:13). He also said, "Say not, When I have leisure I will study; perhaps you will never have leisure" (Aboth 2:5). Jesus said of the Jews, "You search the scriptures" (John 5:39). His invitation to all is "Come learn of me" (Matt. 11:29), and the distinctive term for his follower is *mathētēs* which though translated "disciple" means "pupil." A preacher who is frustrated with himself and whose people are dissatisfied with his efforts could cure this situation if he would make himself a diligent student. The supposition that a pleasing personality and the gift of a glib tongue can take the place of diligent study is one of the occupational hazards of our activity.

E. Elegchein

The preacher's task involves rebuking or convincing (*elegchein*; 2 Tim. 4:2) the wrongdoer. *Elegchein* occurs in the N.T. in eighteen passages. Its corresponding noun form *elegchos* occurs once (Heb. 11:1) and is rendered "conviction." *Elegchein* has at least four varieties of meanings. It means "expose" or "bring to light" (Tit. 2:15). It may mean to convict or convince someone of something as when one is convicted by his conscience (John 8:9; some texts); as when the elder is to convince the gainsayer (Tit. 1:9), and as when Titus is to convince the Cretans (Tit. 1:13). The Holy Spirit convinces the world of sin (John 16:8); and Jude urges that we convince those who doubt (Jude 22; some texts). In some settings *elegchein* has the connotation of correcting or refuting. John the Baptist rebuked Herod for his marriage with Herodias (Luke 3:19). The offending brother is to have his fault shown to him (Matt. 18:15). The wrongdoer is to be reproved (corrected) before all (1 Tim. 5:20; cf. 2 Tim. 4:2). Then the word may suggest punishment or discipline. The Lord reproves those he loves (Rev. 3:19). The dictionary cites no examples of this last category in the work of preachers. As far as the preacher is concerned, this word *elegchein* suggests ideas of persuasion—persuading the wrongdoer that his ways are wrong and that he needs to change his behavior. "To show" or "To make to see" are good colloquial definitions of *elegchein* (cf. Lev. 19:12; Ecclus. 19:13-17). It is a part of bringing every thought into subjection to Christ (2 Cor. 10:5), and must be done by mental and emotional appeals, remembering the proverbial saying "convince a man against his will and he is of the same opinion still." [19]

Titus had been charged "rebuke them sharply" (*elegchein meta pasēs epitagēs*; Tit. 2:15), that is, to act firmly in view of the stubborn character of the Cretan people. His message is from God; he must not be doubtful of his right. His work is to be done *meta pasēs epitagēs*, which is translated into English "with all authority." Though the person who reads only English is tempted to fall into a trap by the use of "with all authority" in this verse in our translations, and may deduce a doctrine of authority for the evangelist, the meaning of *meta pasēs epitagēs* is given by the lexicon[20] as "with all impressiveness." That is a very different concept from that of organic authority.

F. Epitiman

Epitiman ("rebuke," "censure," "speak seriously," or "warn" in order to prevent action) occurs in twenty-eight N.T. passages but with the interesting distribution that all occurrences except two are in the Gospels. Timothy is to "rebuke" (2 Tim. 4:2), and Michael said to the devil, "The Lord rebuke you" (Jude 9). In this second case the idea of "punish" which the word carries in occurrences outside the N.T. is possible.[21]

The import of the word *epitiman* can be seen when Jesus rebukes the demons (Matt. 12:16; Mark 3:12; Luke 4:41; Matt. 17:18; Mark 9:25; Luke 9:42; Mark 1:25; Luke 4:35, 39); when he rebukes the sea (Matt. 8:26; Mark 4:39; Luke 8:24); and in his charge that the disciples not tell that he is the Christ (Matt. 16:20; Mark 8:30; Luke 9:21).

Peter rebukes Jesus when Jesus makes known his approaching death (Matt. 16:22; Mark 8:32, 33); the disciples rebuke the crowd that would bring children to find Jesus (Matt. 19:13; Mark. 10:13; Luke 18:15); the crowd rebukes the blind man who would be healed (Matt. 20:31; Mark 10:48; Luke 18:39); and one thief on the cross rebukes the other (Luke 23:40).

It is of special interest to note that the sinful brother is to be rebuked (Luke 17:3). Like the work of the prophet of the O.T., it is part of the work of the preacher "to declare to Jacob his transgression and to Israel his sin" (Mic. 3:8).[22]

G. Parakalein

The verb *parakalein* and its corresponding noun *paraklēsis* ("encouragement," "exhortation," "comfort," "consolation") are words of many occurrences and many meanings in the N.T. The verb is commonly rendered "exhort" (2 Tim. 4:2); but its meaning includes "invite," "call upon for help," "appeal to," "encourage," "request and implore," "entreat," "console," and "conciliate." The ideas of persuading and encouraging are covered by *parakalein*. The preacher should be a persuader and an encourager—not merely a denouncer.[23]

IV. THE PREACHER AND AUTHORITY

Though the Greek word *exousia* passes into Latin as *auctoritas* and from that source into English as "authority," it is never used in the N.T. for the role of the preacher. The English versions have rendered *epitagēs* as "authority" in one relevant instance: "encourage and rebuke with all authority *(epitagēs)*. Do not let anyone despise you" (Tit. 2:15, NIV). The ASV gave "commandment" as an alternate rendering here for *epitagēs*; and the Bauer lexicon suggests that "with all impressiveness"[24] is the meaning in this case, as we have already pointed out. This passage seems a very weak support for the idea of organic authority for preachers.

Hēgeomai, meaning "to lead" or "guide," occurs in the N.T. only in the present participial form. It is used of men in any leading position. It is used of high officials, of military commanders, and of leaders of religious bodies. Leading men among the brethren

(Judas Barsabbas and Silas) accompanied Paul and Barnabas from Jerusalem with the Apostolic Letter (Acts 15:22). *Hēgemonos* is used of Paul as the chief speaker [of the pair Saul and Barnabas] (Acts 14:12). It is also used in post-apostolic literature as 1 Clement exhorts the Corinthians to be "obedient to your leaders" (1 Clement 1:3) and as Hermas writes, "say to the leaders of the church . . . " (*Vision* 2:2.6; 3:9.9; the form here is *pro-ēgoumenoi*).

Jesus taught that the one leading *(hēgoumenos)* must be as the servant *(diakanos)* (Luke 22:26). The Epistle to the Hebrews does not discuss definite church officials, but does contrast the saints *(hagoi)*—those led—with the *hēgoumenoi* those who lead (Heb. 13:24).[25]

There are certain issues in the translation of *hēgoumenoi* which should be noticed. The KJV rendered Hebrews 13:7 "them which have the rule over you," but gave the marginal alternate "are the guides." We may have ignored the margin because the wording of the text fitted our mind-set. Most of our arguments assume the word "rule." Furthermore, in the KJV the injunction is to give heed to existing rulers as those who had also been their original instructors. The ASV makes the injunction to keep in memory the leaders and teachers who have passed away. The time of the participle is determined by the verb "who spoke" in the sentence. The latter part of the verse ("consider the outcome of their life, and imitate their faith") shows that the ASV is the more correct. Those spoken of are dead and gone, and it is most likely that they were the Apostles who have earlier been spoken of in the Epistle at chapter 2:3.

In 13:17, however, the *hēgoumenoi* are the present leaders; and the exhortation is that they be obeyed *(peithein)* and submitted to *(hupeikein* which occurs only here in the Bible). One should notice that no titles are given for these leaders, either here or in v. 24. The undefined nature of the *hēgoumenoi* leaves the reader open to think of preachers, teachers, or elders. There is a sense in which any of these three is to be obeyed and submitted to; and there are senses in which any of the three of them could be spoken of as keeping watch over souls (Heb. 13:17), though one would more likely think of elders than of the others in this capacity.

Applying this information to the question of the day, the unspecific meaning of *hēgoumenoi* leads men, whether they are arguing for identifying the *hēgoumenoi* with preachers or with elders, to assume the definition they have in mind. Having made that assumption, they can then confirm themselves in contending that their men have the authority they ascribe to them. It is a case of begging the question.

When one considers the question of authority, there is the authority of office, and there is also the authority of respect. There is an authority of truth over error. The words of the preacher who preaches truth carry the authority of truth. Paul speaks of the authority given him for building up, not for tearing down (2 Cor. 10:8). If the preacher will make himself a learned man, he will automatically have the authority that knowledge of the truth carries. People will respect his knowledge. In ancient Judaism the rabbi enjoyed his place of leadership not by appointment to the office but by his great learning. He was in a position of respect; but he considered his learning neither as a crown with which to adorn himself nor as a spade with which to dig—that is, to make a living. The authority of Paul, of Luther, of Wesley, and of Calvin lay in part in their learning.

There is an authority that is exercised through integrity in life as that life reflects the essence of the purity of the Gospel. Without it, all the learning, all the eloquence, and all the grasping for power will be for naught. Ezra came to study the Law, to do it, and to teach its ordinances in Israel (Ezra 7:10). Jesus began "to do and to teach" (Acts 1:1). Paul said, "Follow me as I follow Christ" (1 Cor. 11:1). Phillips Brooks described preaching as the impartation of truth through personality[26]; and were it otherwise, we might try to evangelize the world through tape recorders. The Gospel reflected in life and followed in every action will give more power to the preacher than all his seeking for a place on the right hand or left hand (cf. Matt. 20:21).

There is an authority that comes through genuinely applied love. The person who has completely given himself to the Lord and then to the service of man, pouring out his life and resources, aiding men without restraint in every sort of difficulty will have the power to change the lives of his hearers. Jesus put it, "He who loses his life for my sake will find it" (Matt. 10:39). And another describes the force of love in action: "We love because he first loved us" (1 John 4:19).

One has so well summarized these ideas: "One earns authority through humility, integrity, hard work, quality preaching, meeting the pastoral needs of persons in the congregation, and ability to influence, to a certain degree, the life of the community."[27]

The broken record of human life is "assert, assert, assert"; "be Lord, be Lord, be Lord"; but the call of the Galilean, also handed on through his faithful apostle, is "serve, serve, serve"; "be humble, be humble, be humble"; "be subject, be subject, be subject." After all has been said about the preacher, his function, and his position, he is the slave of a homeless carpenter born in a stable, who lived with no place to lay his head, who rode into Jerusalem on a borrowed donkey, and who was buried in a borrowed tomb.

The slave is not greater than his master (John. 13:16)!

NOTES

[1] L. G. McGreggor, *The Thundering Scot* (Philadelphia: Westminster Press, 1947), p. 226, reports that Regent Morton uttered at Knox's graveside, "Here lies one who neither flattered nor feared any flesh."

[2] C. L. Mitton, *The Epistle to the Ephesians* (Oxford: University Press, 1951), p. 92.

[3] E. G. Selwyn, *The First Epistle of St. Peter* (London: Macmillan, 1955), p. 219.

[4] Isaiah 55:11.

[5] C. H. Dodd, *The Apostolic Preaching and Its Developments* (2d ed., New York and London: Harper & Brothers, 1944), pp. 96ff.

[6] G. Friedrich, *"Euangelion"* in G. W. Bromiley, tr., *Theological Dictionary to the New Testament* (Grand Rapids: Eerdmans, 1964), 2:737.

[7] Eusebius, *Ecclesiastical History* 5.10.2; 3.37.2f.

[8] Hippolytus, *De Antichristo* 56, Tertullian, *Adversus Praxaeus* 21.23.

[9] G. Friedrich, *op. cit.*, 2:736ff.

[10]*Didache* 15:3; *2 Clement* 8:5; Justin Martyr, *Apology* I. 66.3.

[11]Papyrus 66; Irenaeus, *Haeresies* III. 2.10; *Muratorian Canon* 2.

[12]Alan Richardson, *A Theological Wordbook of the Bible* (London: SCM Press, 1956), p. 171.

[13]Walter Bauer, *A Greek-English Lexicon of the New Testament and Other Early Christian Literature*, 2d ed., revised by William F. Arndt, F. Wilbur Gingrich, and Frederick W. Danker (Chicago: University of Chicago Press, 1979, p. 410; J. Schniewind, *"kantangello,"* in G. W. Bromiley, tr., *Theological Dictionary to the New Testament*, (Grand Rapids: Eerdmans, 1964), 2:70-73.

[14]Pliny, "Letter to Trajan" in *Letters and Panegyric*, Letter X. xcvi, 8. Loeb Classical Library (Cambridge: Harvard University Press, 1969), 2:289.

[15]*Didascalia* 3:12, 13; *Apostolic Constitutions* 2:26; 3:15; 8:19, 20, 28; J. G. Davies, "Deacons, Deaconesses and the Minor Orders in the Patristic Period," *Journal of Ecclesiastical History* 14 (April 1963):1-15.

[16]J. Munck, *Paul and the Salvation of Mankind* (Richmond: John Knox Press, 1959), pp. 148-67.

[17]Walter Bauer, *op. cit.*, p. 404; H. Windisch, *"kapēleuō"* in G. W. Bromiley, tr., *op. cit.*, 3:603-5; J. H. Moulton and G. Milligan, *The Vocabulary of the Greek New Testament* (1930; reprinted, Grand Rapids: Eerdmans, 1974), p. 321.

[18]Walter Bauer, *op. cit.*, p. 64.

[19]Ibid., p. 249; F. Buchsel, *"elegchō,"* in G. W. Bromiley, tr., *op. cit.*, 2:473-4; Lawrence J. Lutkemeyer, "The Role of The Paraclete," *Catholic Biblical Quarterly* 8 (April, 1946): 221-3.

[20]Walter Bauer, *op. cit.*, p. 302.

[21]Ibid., p. 303.

[22]E. Stauffer, *"epitimaō"* in G. W. Bromiley, *op. cit.*, 2:623-7.

[23]Walter Bauer, *op. cit.*, p. 662; O. Schmitz, *"parakaleō,"* in G. W. Bromiley, *op. cit.*, 5:793-98.

[24]Ibid., p. 302.

[25]Ibid., p. 344; F. Buchsel, *"hēgeomai,"* etc., in G. W. Bromiley, tr., *op. cit.*, 2:907-9.

[26]Phillips Brooks, *Lectures on Preaching* (N.Y.: E. P. Dutton, 1877), p. 5.

[27]Marvin T. Judy, "As One Having Authority," *Perkins Journal* 30 (Winter, 1979):58ff.

8

Preaching As One Having Authority

The rabbis taught by appeal to authority—the authority of established tradition. They said, "No man creates laws on his own authority." The man with the best memory for what he had heard from scholars was regarded as the best student. Jesus, however, made no appeal to the tradition but taught as one having authority in his own right. His message was not his own but was that of him who sent him. Paul claimed guidance of the Spirit and insisted that his Gospel had the authority of God back of it (1 Cor. 14:37; Gal. 1:11-12).

The preacher of God's word today needs to speak as one having authority. "If the trumpet gives an uncertain sound, who shall prepare for the battle?" (1 Cor. 14:8). But from whence shall he get that authority?

When one preaches, he may still speak with the authority of tradition as did the Pharisees. He may hand on those things which his parents taught him. He may give special attention to "what our position has always been." Such is not bad if parents and teachers happen to have taught him the truth. All of us accept many things from those who went before. However, such an authority is actually identical with that claimed by the Pharisees for the Oral Law and that claimed by the Catholics for tradition.

One may hand on what he has read in the accepted commentaries. I, as you, have sat in classes where every question was answered by reading from a trusted commentary. People thought they were "just studying the Bible" when in reality, they were studying B. W. Johnson, Adam Clarke, and Albert Barnes. We usually accept from the commentaries those things that are congenial to the opinions we have already formed. With the conflicting voices of our world, how is the follower of tradition to distinguish which tradition he is to follow?

When one preaches, he may speak with the authority of dogmatism. Of one person someone commented, "He has just enough education to be certain that he knows everything." We are so constructed that the things we do not know do not bother us greatly. A man's need for training may be obvious to everyone except himself. But there is a difference between dogmatism and truth.

The preacher cannot preach with the authority of the inspired man. His authority must be the authority which comes from "I know." In dealing with the Word which God has given, by study and investigation one must weigh that which is false against that which is true and find it wanting. Students often fill their papers with appeal to the authorities. They seem to think that "Bultmann says this, Cullmann says that, and some other 'man' says the other; and far be it from me to question such scholars as these," solves problems. I always insist that no paper is correctly constructed until one has studied the topic thoroughly enough that he can with confidence say "I know." Shouting, hammering the pulpit, and stamping the feet do not give authority to what one says.

In moments of truth all of us who preach would be forced to admit that we have sometimes unintentionally handed on mis-information for truth. We have been careful in what we call "doctrine," but in the peripheral matters we have not been sure whether we had facts or fiction. While none will attain to complete knowledge, by a life of study the preacher diminishes the areas in which his statements border on ignorance.

Wisdom and learning are not to be equated with each other. The educated fool remains a fool. Wisdom comes from natural endowment and from experience. But no man's judgment is better than the facts he possesses. Dictators regularly take away the freedom of the press in order that men may not have access to the facts they need in order to make right judgments. The ordinary Christian—and how much more the preacher—is commanded to grow in knowledge. Correct education supplies information, but it also provides training in correct processes of thought.

I categorically reject the sentiment one hears expressed now and then which suggests that there is a necessary antithesis between scholarship and preaching. Says one, "We are training preachers and not scholars." Says another, "There are some scholars who just cannot preach."

By general consent J. W. McGarvey is the most capable scholar the Restoration Movement has produced. His one hundred year old commentary on the Book of Acts continues to be standard among us despite all the archaeological finds which were not accessible to McGarvey. Along with his scholarship McGarvey was recognized as a capable preacher. People elected to hear McGarvey because his sermons never disappointed them.

Men vary widely in their native ability. One could have showered upon me all the musical training the world offers and I still would never have been a Beethoven; unlimited art training would not have made me into a Michelangelo. Some men have outstanding ability in preaching while others do not. No amount of training will give the man ability who is not endowed with it. There are untrained men who cannot preach just as there are trained men who cannot. If I have only limited success in preaching, the basic fault is not that I have been exposed to education.

Some men in every field of endeavor and in every generation are outstanding with only a minimum of formal training. But they are not untrained; by self-discipline they have trained themselves. Training is to enable a man to take what ability he has and to do more with it than he would otherwise have been able to do. There is no logical reason why a man should spend a major portion of his life in learning on his own what he could be taught by a teacher in a relatively short time. Franklin said, "Experience keeps a dear school, but fools learn in no other."

"For Ezra had set his heart to study the law of the Lord, and to do it, and to teach his statutes and ordinances in Israel" (Ezra 7:10).

This is what gives authority to preaching.

9

The Majority of the Men?

Men universally tend to draw analogies from their culture and to understand their Biblical duties in the light of these analogies. History is replete with examples of how men imposed their institutions upon their understanding of the Bible; and our age is no exception. In local congregations with no elders, there is a widespread conviction that the majority of the men should rule, because majority rule is the sort of political government we know and admire. Once men have accepted the presupposition that the majority of the men constitute an authority, they can justify whatever they will do, even if it is a coup of the most vicious sort.

It is the duty of every Christian "to be eager to maintain the unity of the spirit in the bond of peace" (Eph. 4:3). He is commanded by the Lord "to seek the things that make for peace" (Rom. 14:19). He as an individual is commanded by the Lord "If possible, so far as it depends upon you, live peaceably with all" (Rom. 12:18). These are not optional matters; they are duties that are incumbent upon all, whether or not there are elders. All ought to be chiefly interested in these duties. The individual's desires and preferences should be subordinated to a concern for the welfare of the body of Christ.

The New Testament church acted "with one accord" (Acts 1:4; 2:1, 46; 4:24; 5:12). When early Christians had a problem, they arrived at one accord (Acts 15:25) and then acted on the problem. The Philippian church is ordered by Paul to be "of one accord" (Phil. 2:2). Biblical authority comes by a direct command, an approved example, or by a necessary inference. The Biblical position for the action of the church is that it acted "with one accord." This position is required both by Biblical command and Biblical example.

Now it may readily be granted that a group of people may decide that they wish to follow the leadership of selected men in their number. And it is further granted that many congregations are operated that way with whatever minority there may be in them submitting graciously or otherwise to the will of the majority. Business is transacted in the general business meeting. But this practice is entirely in the realm of expediency and is not in the realm of Biblical command, example, or necessary inference at all. It could just as well be done in some other way (e.g., informal polling of wishes of the people; foregoing action to which there is opposition) if that other way could enable the congregation to act "with one accord." There is not one syllable in the Bible that describes the details of how a congregation arrives at a decision for action whether it be by casting lots, by flipping a coin, by voting, or whatever.

Leadership in the New Testament is really leadership by the consent of those led. It is a wise leader who leads where his flock wants to go. An elder is to lead, "not as domineering . . . but being an example to the flock" (1 Pet. 5:2). While he (as other older men) is not to be rebuked, but is to be exhorted as a father (1 Tim. 5:1), it is also envisioned that a charge might be made against him. Such charges must be established at the mouth of two or three witnesses (1 Tim. 5:19)—the legal number in Jewish law.

When one suggests that a congregation should act "with one accord," it goes without saying that such action must be in keeping with Biblical teaching in matters on which the Bible has spoken. If men become determined to do error, the servant of God must oppose the error, even if he stands as lonely as Elijah envisioned himself to stand. But even where other matters are under consideration, one immediately encounters the objection, "If we only acted 'with one accord,' we would never be able to do anything." This objection asks the wrong question first. The first question is, "Do we have the Biblical duty to act with one accord?" If we do have the Biblical duty (and the above cited passages establish that we do), then we should seek ways to conform regardless of how difficult the task. This is the attitude we should take toward any duty the Bible imposes upon us. Self-control also is a difficult task, but we must be self-controlled however difficult it may be.

The basic question of how a congregation can act with one accord is, of course, crucial. We Americans are activists and feel that we must get things done. We all tend to be the "now generation." But patience and charity can help a congregation to be in one accord. In six months men often see things differently from the way they do at the moment. A delay for a period of study and prayer might in some matters bring us together. An effort to persuade is of an entirely different character from an effort to force. Often a bad spirit is the chief deterrent to unified action. This problem is one of attitude, not of form of government, and can only be cured by study, repentance, and prayer. Even the decision of a properly constituted eldership will not bring "one accord" where attitudes are bad. Compromises might bring us together; hence, where men are at loggerheads, it may be in order to seek alternative actions. In some instances, mediation of tension might help. Paul asked, "Can it be that there is no man among you wise enough to decide between members of the brotherhood?" (1 Cor. 6:5). Paul's question implies that the judgment of such a wise brother should be followed.

A congregation can act with one accord by each member keeping himself conscious that the Christian is not to be contentious (Rom. 2:8; 1 Cor. 11:16; Tit. 3:10); that he is not to be

77

quarrelsome (2 Tim. 2:24); that the wisdom from above is pure, peaceable, and open to reason (James 3:17); that each is to count the other better than himself (Phil. 2:3). Of course, there is a problem here, for no man ever classified himself as contentious, and men are quick so to label the man who holds opposing views to the views of the majority.

Rather than the majority imposing its will on the minority, Paul's teaching on the attitude to be taken in the matter of eating meats (1 Cor. 8: 1ff.) would suggest the need to yield so-called "rights" in the interest of the welfare of the weak brother. This might suggest precedent for the majority yielding to the minority in some situations. The apostles delegated responsibility to the dissidents in the matter of neglect of the Grecian widows and maintained peace (Acts 6:1ff.). These suggestions are expedients and are not to be insisted on to the disruption of the peace of the congregation. The task of acting "with one accord" is not easy, but it could make for peace in many places where there is strife.

The duty to act "with one accord" has been established by both Biblical command and example. What Biblical passage, however, remotely suggests that a group of people, large or small, has the Biblical right to constitute themselves into a governing body over the Lord's congregation, to impose their will upon the remainder of the congregation without regard to congregational feeling?

One says, "I have always heard that in the absence of elders, the majority of the men should rule the congregation." Now "I have always heard" does not constitute Biblical authority for any practice. Another says, "That is the way I think it should be." "I think" does not constitute Biblical authority. Now, back to our question, what verse of Scripture authorizes the majority of the men to presume to constitute themselves into the authority in the church? No such verse exists. There is no Biblical precedent for such action.

Except for the two letters to Timothy and the one letter to Titus, which are letters to individuals, and except for isolated charges to other individuals, Paul addresses his letters to the church—not to a group within the church. There is no case in which he charges "the majority of the men" to take action. There is no case in which he commissions the majority of the church to take action, nor any case in which he commissions the minority. He charges the church.

The word "majority" does not occur in the English Bible (King James Version) at all—not to mention its occurrence to describe a governing body for the Lord's church. Across history the majority has been wrong about as many times as it has been right. A majority brought on the flood; a majority sold Joseph into Egypt (a majority of ten to one, by the way); a majority report of ten to two of the spies kept Israel in the wilderness forty years; a majority crucified Jesus; a majority stoned Stephen; a majority beat Paul in the synagogues; a majority burned witches in Salem; and a majority slaughtered six million Jews in Germany.

There is not one word in the Bible which suggests that a majority of any sort can presume to set themselves up as a ruling body in the Lord's church. There is not one word which suggests that a minority (this word also is not in the Bible) can set themselves up over the Lord's church. Not even an elder is to be a lord over God's heritage (1 Pet. 5:3). That being true, how much more is it unsuitable for any lesser figures to be so? The Biblical precept is that the church act "with one accord."

In the absence of a passage setting forth "the majority of the men" as an authority, the struggle often seen to establish this situation in the congregations takes on aspects of "might makes right." Might never did make right, and it does not in this situation. Jesus said, "You know that the rulers of the Gentiles lord it over them, and their great men exercise authority over them. It shall not be so among you" (Matt. 20:25, 26).

As Jesus made very plain in Matthew 20:25, 26, you do not become great in the kingdom of God by seizing and exercising power. You become great by rendering service. If you will distinguish yourself for your Christian graces and by the outstanding Christian service you render, you will not have to seize power. The Lord's people will willingly follow you wherever the Word of God leads; they can, with patience, be persuaded in matters of expediency; and God will be glorified by the life you live.

79

10

Tradition

JESUS AND THE PHARISEES

The chief conflicts of Jesus were those with the Pharisees. These people, of whom Josephus says there was a total of 6,000 in the first century, considered themselves to be the church within the church—the most righteous group—of the Jewish nation. Paul said, "After the strictest sect of our religion I lived a Pharisee" (Acts 26:5). The thing that made a man a Pharisee was his belief that at Mount Sinai God not only gave the written law, but also gave the oral law which had been preserved in an unbroken chain from generation to generation—Moses, Joshua, the Elders, the men of the Great Synagogue, and the pairs of teachers—until Jesus' day. The oral teaching was considered equally binding with the written law. The Sadducees, in contrast, rejected the oral law and consequently rejected belief in angels and spirits and the resurrection of the dead.

Actually the oral law (called the "traditions of the elders" in Gospels), instead of being from Moses, represented the crystalization and codification of custom. Passing generations found it desirable to define and clarify obscurities in the Law. The Law said you should not work on the Sabbath. The Pharisees attempted to define work so that men would know clearly what was forbidden and what was permitted. The Law said you should not go out of your place on the Sabbath. The Pharisees defined a Sabbath Day's journey. The motivation of these rules, as the Pharisees saw them, was "to keep men far from transgression." That is, there is a line at which one passes from righteousness over into sin. The Pharisees were attempting so to regulate life that men would not come near that line. Their case is the perfect example of how people of good motives can go astray.

Jesus had no conflict with the Pharisees over the written Law. He was born under the Law and he lived by it, for he came not to destroy the Law, but to fulfill it. His clashes with them were over eating with unwashed hands, plucking grain on the Sabbath, and healing on the Sabbath—all matters that came under regulation of the oral law. When challenged because his disciples ate with unwashed hands, Jesus turned the tables by accusing the Pharisees of transgressing the laws of God because of their traditions. His illustration is the matter of honoring father and mother (see Matt. 15:3-6).

Whatever else may be involved in honoring father and mother, it is obvious from this passage that Jesus understood it to mean providing for them in their need. Paul also understood this to be an obligation of caring for aged relatives and said that the one who neglected to provide for his own had denied the faith (1 Tim. 5:8). But Pharisaic tradition said, if a man says "Corban," he is freed from the duty. Excavators at the Wailing Wall in Jerusalem have recently found the Hebrew word "Korban" inscribed on a jar. It is a word that means sacrifice. In the Gospels it would seem that the man was in substance saying, "My property has been sacrificed (or dedicated) to the Lord. Therefore, I have nothing left with which to take care of my parents." In this way he escaped the obligation.

TRADITION ITSELF NOT WRONG

It is easy from this episode to jump to the conclusion that Jesus condemned religious tradition per se: The Pharisees accepted tradition and Jesus was against all tradition. But a second look will reveal to you that Jesus himself did many things for which the only authority is tradition. He had a custom of attending the synagogue, but the synagogue and its worship are traditional. No mention is made of the synagogue in the Law or in the entire Old Testament. Giving thanks before eating food is traditional as also is the custom of singing a hymn at the end of the Passover observance. There must be something more at stake in the controversy than just tradition versus commandment.

It is not unusual for us to get a general concept but to be a little unclear on it. When a little out of focus, we may think that other people have religious traditions but that we just go by the Bible. But unless we had someone whose task was to see that we always do things differently from the way we did them before, it is inevitable that we develop customs, and customs prolonged are traditions.

A friend and I were walking down the street of an eastern city and came upon a church building that had a sign: "Church of the Messiah." "What is wrong with that?" he asked me. "Nothing, but you had better not erect that type of sign if you do not want a squawk on your hands," I replied. "We do not do it that way" is a pretty strong argument in all circles.

We all know that the "necessary inference" category gives us authority for a number of practices but the "how" under this category tends to become custom. We have a special building and a certain type of worship—is that Biblical or traditional? Our chairs face a speaker who uses a pulpit to speak from—Biblical or traditional? A man directs the singing and we sing out of special hymn books—Biblical or traditional? We pass the communion tray down the pew and pass a collection plate for the collection. Is the manner of procedure Biblical or traditional? Songs, prayer, preaching, and communion—what about the order and amount of time devoted to each of them? A worship service at set hours of the morning; two services on Sunday and one on Wednesday night—Biblical or traditional? You probably have laughed at Jim Bill McInteer's story of the man sitting on the front row who indicated that he wanted to be baptized and the preacher said to him, "Would you mind stepping back a few steps so that you can come forward and make the confession?" We read a Bible bound in black leather with red or gold edges, and quite a howl went up when someone came out with a hardback red-covered Bible. Is the appearance of the Bible Biblical or traditional? Use of a particular English version of Scripture is traditional. I was visiting a short time back and met a man whose favorite expression to meet a new suggestion was, "You are killing cows in India." Well, tradition creates quite a few sacred cows, but you just cannot feature a people existing over any time without developing some traditions or customs.

THE ISSUES ON TRADITION

What are the issues on this question of tradition? First, a clear distinction is to be made between traditions of men and the traditions of the Gospel. "Tradition" (*paradosis*) merely means that which is handed down. It can be used in a good sense as well as in a bad sense. Paul handed down that which he received (1 Cor. 11:23) and the Corinthians received it (1 Cor. 15:1) so that they had received a tradition. He condemned those who do not walk after the tradition they have received (2 Thess. 3:6), and exhorted others to hold fast to the traditions (2 Thess. 2:15; 1 Cor. 11:2). It is right to follow the traditions of the Gospel, but Paul also warns those who are deceived by human tradition rather than following Christ (Col. 2:8).

Second, we will consider binding traditions on men versus doing things traditionally. When Judaizers wanted to force men to be circumcised, James spoke of tempting God by binding on them a yoke which neither we nor our fathers were able to bear (Acts 15:10). Paul saw nothing wrong in circumcising Timothy, but would not allow Titus to be forced. If a man wants to increase the fish business on Friday, that seems innocent enough until he starts saying that I have to do it also or that I would be better in the sight of God if I did. The church is not a club where we draw up rules of membership and of life and then guarantee that people will go to heaven by keeping them. To do so is to come pretty close to tempting God.

84

Ours is the age of the promoter. Major commands of the Gospel are generic in nature leaving us room to devise how they are to be carried out. The Gospel must go to every creature, but how? The autonomy of the New Testament congregations allows any person who thinks he has a good idea to promote it among us, and a high percentage of the ideas being promoted are good works in my judgment and worthy of support. A Christian ought to be ready to every good work. But suppose I should have misgivings about the wisdom of a particular project (popular as it might be) or suppose, while approving the general idea of the project, I should have misgivings about the capabilities of the particular promoter to accomplish his project, am I the less a Christian for it? Should he consider me as his enemy?

Walter Scott, the well-known teacher in the early Restoration Movement, taught us that there are five steps in the plan of salvation: hear, believe, repent, confess, and be baptized. I am sure that summary has five steps because people have five fingers. If people had been four fingered, Scott would have come up with a four point summary. But he put the essentials of the Gospel so that people could remember them and for its purpose it would be hard to improve on. How many times an adverse word about someone's pet project has touched off an atomic explosion in the church! Now if you do not climb on the band wagon of whatever Lewis is promoting, it is obvious that you are seriously lacking in depth of insight and judgment! I learned a long time ago that the mathematicians loved math and that the counselors thought counseling would solve our problems. But was Scott right that there are five steps in the plan of salvation or should he have really said there are six: hear, believe, repent, confess, be baptized, and be gung-ho on cassette evangelism, Gospel blimp, deeper life, telephone counseling, pre-dawn training, Mud Flat school, or whatever else is riding high at the moment?

Traditions may be innocent enough, but when they become duties, they take on an entirely different character. I am convinced that most of us could profitably give some attention to distinctions between the Gospel and our traditions that collect like moss on a tree about it. Traditions need to be recognized as traditions and not be made into binding beliefs and practices.

Third, we should guard against traditions that conflict with the Word of God. The real conflict of Jesus with the Pharisees was due to the fact that traditions have an innate tendency sooner or later to crystallize into conflict with duties of the Word of God. The **Corban** tradition, which Jesus mentioned, released men from the duty to care for their parents. The Sabbath prohibitions overlooked weightier matters of the Law, namely that human need comes ahead of ritual.

In a parallel way, (a) the tradition of baptizing babies frees people from recognition of the duty to believe and be baptized; (b) religious holidays not only bind men where God has not bound (Gal. 4:10), but obscure the duty to observe the first day of the week; (c) religious party names are divisive and cause a neglect of glorifying God in the name Christian; (d) some organizational practices throw into neglect leadership by elders in the Lord's churches; (e) types of worship can encourage men to be satisfied with less than New Testament worship.

CONCLUSION

Certainly the Gospel contains its many commands which you cannot afford to neglect. It has its prohibitions which you must heed. They are absolute, forbidding the works of the flesh. There are some examples—as gathering for the breaking of bread— which you would not ignore. But the details of many other practices are traditional. Yet observe how the change of any of them disturbs us. The disturbance may be caused because we do not know Scripture well enough to distinguish between the command and the custom; or it may disturb us because we have never before raised the question for ourselves into which category the practice fits. We need to keep beliefs and practices in the proper focus. We need to be a people who by reason of use have their senses exercised to discern that which is good and that which is evil.

11

Reflections on Preaching

We are all interested in one common goal of influencing as many people as we can for good for our Lord. We all share a common problem that there are more demands on our time than we can meet. Hence, a system of priorities has to be set up that must be continuously reevaluated across the course of our lives. We must ask, "How can I make my efforts count for the most?" When we have made that choice for ourselves, others about us may dispute its validity. We do not see ourselves as others see us.

The local preacher, in particular, is confronted with this problem. Where is the priority to be given? Is it to study? Is it to sermon preparation? Is it to counseling? Is it to community involvement? Is it to mass media? Is it to socializing? Is it to bulletin preparation? All of these activities, and many others, are knocking on the preacher's door for their share of his time; something can be said in favor of each of them; and some matter of personal judgment is involved in any ranking of them in importance in achieving the goal of influencing people for good.

Teaching the techniques of preaching is not one of the areas in which I claim to be an expert; nevertheless, among the voices that are attempting to tell you what you ought to do, I would like to speak a word about some of my concerns.

VISITATION

First, I would like to speak in behalf of what seems to be a dying art—the ministerial call. It has died because most of the people in our congregations are too busy at their work or at their television sets to want to take time out to talk to the preacher. It has died because the preacher, himself, is too busy to give it a high ranking place in his priorities. It went out with the "house call" of the physician. Many preachers have adopted this policy: If you want to see me, you can make an appointment in my office at my office hours. Not very many preachers, particularly in our larger congregations, do a lot of calling. We also have to admit that we are not changing the lives of any startling number of people in our congregations.

An older preacher under whom I studied preaching years ago insisted that a local preacher should be in the home of every family in his congregation at least twice a year every year he was with the congregation. I do not know any preacher who does that; I confess that I never did it, for after I heard him, I was always a student or teacher and was doing "fill in" Sunday preaching. That teacher related in the class an admonition his mother had given him when he was a beginning preacher: "If you stay in a congregation for any time there is not a family in it in which there will not be a tragedy of some sort, and at that time you will want to go to help that family as a trusted friend—not as a stranger."

I would not at all say that if you, in your work, have neglected to go to your people until tragedy strikes that you should stay away—but how awkward it is to find yourself at the door of a house where you have never been before and there has been a death! How awkward to go and introduce yourself to sorrowing people who do not know you and whom you do not know! How little you can accomplish in contrast with what you could have done if you were already that one to whom they turned for spiritual support in their need!

Some churches have an active visitation program conducted by the elders; others have an associate minister who is responsible for visitation needs; and in some cases the arrangements work quite well. Sick people do get visited; the weak and the grieving do get encouraged. The elders may be quite willing for you not to visit. But there is one aspect of preaching that someone else's visiting cannot fill. It cannot put you into the lives of the people so that you can motivate them to be a different people! You may not be able to accomplish that in many cases even when you are in their lives, but at least you are in a much better position to try.

In preaching there is a great need for the well-prepared and capably delivered sermon; but we who preach need also to keep asking, "What is the purpose of the sermon?" In the ultimate (whether one is doing evangelistic preaching or edifying preaching), the changing of lives of the hearers is the goal. One does that as much by what he is and by his relationship with the individual, as by what he says. An enthusiastic response from the audience at the door at the end of the sermon may fall far short of that goal. The Lord told the prophet Ezekiel that he appeared to his people as "one who sings love songs with a beautiful voice and plays well on an instrument, for they hear what you say, but they will not do it" (Ezek. 32:32). That can also be true of any preacher. He can be extremely popular and his people not be one whit changed when he is through.

A great deal of preaching one listens to is well presented and deals with at least semi-Biblical themes, but the man in the pew goes away no different from the condition in which he came; his emotions have not been stirred, his heart has not been melted. The preaching did not deal with a problem he was actively wrestling with nor did it convince him that he should start wrestling with one he had previously neglected.

It is very easy for us who preach to turn our eyes to the ends of the earth. We can see evangelistic opportunities where we are not, and we can imagine success in programs that do not fit our situation.

89

We can dream of reaching the billions, when we are not reaching the tens; and we can become so enthralled with that idea that our time becomes too valuable in our estimation to bother with individuals. But we must never forget that though on some occasions Jesus spoke to five thousand or to four thousand, he also called a few men out of their fishing boats and worked in depth with them. He met with Nicodemus at night, he talked with the woman at the well, he was in the home of Mary, Martha, and Lazarus. He called Zacchaeus out of the tree and went home with him.

HUMOR

Another concern which I have is with humor. No one has a better appreciation for well-turned humor than I do. I have been known to tell a stale joke or so now and then. We all know its value in getting the attention of a sleepy audience. However, a question of balance enters. Some time ago, I went to a revival conducted by a speaker of national reputation. His sermon was to a large extent made up of a series of jokes with a short admonition at the end of the whole. I came away wondering about his reputation. Is preaching an after-dinner occasion? I thought of Milton's *Lycidas*, "The hungry sheep look up and are not fed."

Areas of humor merit some thought. It is easy to feel very clever in your jokes and to provoke a great laugh out of a large part of an audience while driving a sword into the heart of some you should be trying to influence for good. One person in about five in America will suffer some emotional derangement during his life. Jokes at the expense of the mentally and emotionally deranged cease to be funny when you have so suffered or when someone near you has so suffered. Is your joke worth forfeiting permanently the possibility of helping these people? People do not forgive sword jabs to their hearts.

Drunkenness and the antics of the intoxicated present humorous situations to those removed from the problem. But, the sickness (or sin, as you will) of drunkenness is not humorous to the family suffering from the effects of alcoholism. There is nothing funny about the behavior of a drunken father, a drunken mother, or a drunken child. The preacher's joke is not going to lighten the burden of the wife trying in desperation to hold a marriage together with a drunken husband, or of a husband trying to live with an alcoholic wife.

Death is a light matter to those far from it and is the subject of a great deal of humor. But death ceases to be a funny matter when the doctor announces to someone near you, "You have a malignancy," or "You have a crucial heart problem and may drop dead at any time." It is not funny when one near you has recently gone. No one can tell you about that. You have to walk that path yourself to know. There is not an audience to which you will speak in which there is not one or more whose world is shattered and whose heart is breaking over an irreparable loss it has suffered. Is a laugh worth a sword thrust to open again the wound of that bleeding heart? Surely we who want to change lives can find something more appropriate about which to be funny. I would suggest that the preacher who is concerned about his influence should make for himself an infallible rule: "I will be sensitive to the feelings of *all* my people! I will not needlessly wound the hearts of those I am seeking to win."

MOTIVATION OR LEARNING?

Yet another concern is over what is supposed to happen in a sermon. It is a question over which we might have a lot of discussion. A brother, speaking rather unkindly of the efforts of his preacher, said, "You have to park your brain with your car on the parking lot each Sunday before you go in." Is there supposed to be intellectual stimulation in preaching? At an earlier time the preacher was the best informed man in the community. That has long ceased to be. A preacher here in Memphis some time ago said, "All you need to preach are a few scriptures and the gift of gab."

It is likely a false dichotomy to oppose motivation and information. I think that in preaching, motivation must grow out of the information that is supplied. At the carnival one buys cotton candy which is a pinch of sugar fluffed up; but he does not get very much in the fluff. Motivation without information is only stirring zeal without knowledge. It is all fluff. One can attend and respond to only so many spiritual pep rallies. If there is no substance, after a while he ceases to respond. Aesop told of the boy who cried, "Wolf, Wolf!" until no one listened when the wolf really came. In my opinion if the audience is not getting something besides a shot of enthusiasm, in fairly short order, the shot will no longer stimulate.

I listened to a preacher some years ago with whose basic theological orientation I am not sympathetic. He chose the statements about Elijah in James chapter 5 as his text. He began by telling of having seen a movie depicting figures of early American history in which the shortcomings of Washington, Franklin, Adams, and the other leaders were laid bare, but which at least magnified what uncommon things these ordinary men had achieved in building the American Republic. He moved to "Elijah, a man of like passion with us," and he said, "Elijah was afraid, as I am afraid;" "Elijah became discouraged as I get discouraged." "Elijah was short on faith as I am short on faith." But then he also told of Elijah's great opposition to Jezebel, turning the tide of Baal worship in Israel. As I listened to that familiar story which I have known since childhood, something happened that has seldom happened in listening to preaching. I suddenly found myself thinking, if God could do that with a man like Elijah, who knows, maybe, in spite of everything, he might be able to do some small thing with Jack Lewis.

That is what preaching is all about!

12

That Which Every Joint Supplies

On the American frontier, the single individual surrounded by an untamed forest, by wild animals, and by hostile savages, was doomed; but by forming a community to which he contributed his part, he gained safety and ultimately tamed the wilderness, built roads and cities, and developed America.

A man and a woman pool their abilities to form a home, each contributing to its existence, but out of the relationship receiving far more than they contribute, accomplishing together what neither could do alone.

Paul envisioned the church in these terms as he compared it to an efficiently functioning human body. Each member of the body carries on its function and in turn lives from the life which flows from the body. The body exists through that which each joint supplies (Eph. 4:16), but each joint lives through that which the body supplies. An arm separated from the body will quickly die. One can readily see that a body which has legs that will not function, ears that will not hear, and eyes that cannot see is greatly handicapped.

On the other hand, when every part of the body is functioning normally, what a marvel the human body is, and how great it is to be alive! Of the church, Paul said, "The body, when each part is working properly, makes bodily growth and upbuilds itself in love" (Eph. 4:16).

Jesus plainly taught that "the laborer deserves his food" (Matt. 10:10). Paul expressed the same idea when he said, "Those who proclaim the gospel should get their living by the gospel" (1 Cor. 9:14). It is altogether right that the congregations should support men both at home and abroad to carry on the various ministries. No person can rightfully object to the church's paying those persons who devote full time to its work.

But professionalism is all too easy to develop. In some denominational churches the singing is carried on by paid musicians who in many cases may not even believe the teachings of that particular religious group. I have known of preachers who preached for denominations to which they did not belong and whose doctrine they did not believe. It was a livelihood for them, or it enabled them to live on a higher plane than they could otherwise have done. Our economy tempts us to hire more and more services, to expect to take care of all situations with our dollars, and to put less and less of our time and talents at the Lord's disposal.

Among us a fixed group of services to the congregation carry with them a financial remuneration, while other services do not. While in my opinion a congregation would be entirely on scriptural ground if it decided that it needed full-time elders, the work of an elder is ordinarily not a remunerative position. These men place their time and ability at the congregation's disposal. At times a man who has retired from his business can devote himself full time to the Lord's work as an elder without financial remuneration (1 Tim. 5:17).

An elder, when inviting me to address the congregation, in an apologetic way informed me, "We do not pay a person who is in the congregation for being guest speaker on Sunday night." Sunday morning was, of course, another matter. If a person is a member of the congregation, has his own living, and no expense is involved in

94

his speaking, why the difference? When I was newer in the congregation, an elder asked me about teaching a special class for teachers, and then embarrassed me by saying, "Some of the men were wondering if you would expect to be paid."

The people who teach in the educational program of a congregation all contribute their services to the congregation as a part of their service to the Lord who entrusted them with teaching ability. If a person has such ability, what better way can he serve the Lord than to teach? I have no scorn for the person who finds his place in the Lord's work in cutting the grass, parking cars, passing the collection plate, attending committee meetings or even knocking on doors. If these are the things that one can do, then he should do them. Personally, I feel that my time is better spent in preparing lessons and in presenting them. The teacher who carefully prepares and teaches both on Sunday morning and on Wednesday night is contributing a sizable block of his time to the program. His service is no greater than those who serve in a less public way, but he is exercising his talent.

No less service is rendered by the other ministries of the congregation. These are the bus drivers, the people who do visitation persuading people to ride the buses, and those who teach and maintain order in the bus programs. There are those who do the printing, count the money, keep the records, look after the library, visit the sick, and a host of other services. All of these people have their living provided by secular jobs. They could "moonlight" and increase their income to provide better cars, houses, and clothes. But in their service to the church they have found a way to put their talent to work for the Lord, laying up a good store for the days to come.

However, the unused abilities in any of our congregations, compared with those which we use, make the church the world's number one inefficient institution. Any business venture would fail if it harnessed only the percentage of ability at its command as does the church. Many a Christian devotes a major portion of his time to service organizations because he has found no way to find himself a place in the church's program. Many a lady whiles away her time at the soap operas or on the bridge circuit because she has found nothing to challenge her talent. In some cases we hire musicians when we have sitting in the pews musicians of equal attainment who have found no way to put their ability into the Lord's service.

The dissatisfaction a person has with a congregation decreases in inverse proportion to the amount of time that he devotes to its programs. Sitting on the pew is important activity. When not inspired by the lesson, not moved by the songs, one is voting for what the church stands for and for the sort of activity it carries on by his presence. But pew sitting does not fill a basic need in mankind. Men were granted the privilege of work at the creation. The miserable man is the person who is not justifying the space he occupies by meaningful work. On the other hand, the person who has found a task worth pouring himself into has the key to most of life's problems. It solves his boredom, it solves his recreation problem, it solves his self-centeredness.

If the church paid all those who participate in its programs, they would doubtless have better houses, lands, food, and clothing. But there would be no money left for charity, for building programs, for mission work, and for evangelism. One of the great statements made by John F. Kennedy was, "Do not ask what your country can do for you; ask what you can do for your country." We sing about the church: "For her my prayers ascend; for her my tears shall fall." Cannot these tears be accompanied by hours spent in useful service? If every person who has a living already could be brought to see the church as a place where he freely puts his talent to work for the Lord, it would free thousands of dollars for carrying the Gospel to the lost.

"The whole body, joined and knit together by every joint with which it is supplied, when each part is working properly, makes bodily growth and upbuilds itself in love" (Eph. 4:16).

How about you?

13

When God Says, "You Are Unworthy!"

A man's personal dreams and ambitions and the role God has for him are not necessarily the same. Our personal estimation of our abilities and of our suitability for a position we want may not correspond with the estimation of those responsible for filling that position. To our great disappointment, we may be passed by and another person chosen. Despite our ambitions, our associates may feel that the aims of the organization will be better served by one we consider inferior to ourselves. While we are seeing ourselves as ten-talented men, our associates may see us as only one-talented men.

The providence of God must operate through the choices boards make for administrators and through the decisions those administrators make as they fill their positions. In a democracy it has to work through democratic processes. This does not mean that all the choices are right; time sometimes demonstrates that unworthy men gain public office; that an unqualified man has been selected to be an elder; that elders have selected the wrong preacher; that the wrong teacher has been selected for a class; and that men of better qualifications have been passed over for less suitable men. But through it all God must over-rule the evil men do; God must work for good to those who love him (Rom. 8:28).

WHAT SEEMS GOOD TO HIM

When God had found Eli's sons unworthy to be judges over Israel, he informed Samuel in the night that the guilt of Eli's house would never be expiated. Though the boy Samuel feared to speak out, under Eli's insistent demand, Samuel told him God's plans. Eli replied, "It is the Lord; let him do what seems good to him" (1 Sam. 3:18).

When God rejected the house of Saul and selected David to be king over Israel, the men who lost most in the choice were Saul's sons. The kingship would not be theirs. But Jonathan said to David, "You will be king over Israel and I will be next to you" (1 Sam. 23:17). Jonathan became the buffer between Saul and David. Saul harshly denounced him for not having ambition and for aiding a rival. The Lord said "no" to any personal ambitions Jonathan may have had; but there was no rivalry, no envy between him and David.

John the Baptist was sent by the Lord to be forerunner, to prepare the way of the Lord. His role was a secondary one. To questioners he openly said, "I am not the Christ," "I am not Elijah," "I am not a prophet." "I am the voice of one crying in the wilderness, make straight the way of the Lord" (John 1:20ff.). It was John who said: "I am not the Christ, but I have been sent before him. He who has the bride is the bridegroom; the friend of the bridegroom, who stands and hears him, rejoices greatly at the bridegroom's voice; therefore, this joy of mine is now full. He must increase, but I must decrease" (John 3:28-30).

These great men had learned that lesson which is so hard for most of us to learn—a lesson stated in the Psalms, "The Lord will fulfill his purpose for me" (Ps. 57:2; 138:8). The idea was further stated by Peter, "Humble yourselves therefore under the mighty hand of God, that in due time he may exalt you" (1 Pet. 5:6).

Who would deny that it is easier for us to affirm that lesson when our personal ambitions and desires have been realized than when we have been frustrated again and again? Who would deny that he has been ready for exaltation before the Lord was ready to exalt him? When, as it were, we want to go into Bithynia (Acts 16:17) and the "Spirit of Jesus" does not allow it, it is a lot harder to respond, "It is the Lord; let him do what seems good to him."

WHAT SEEMS GOOD TO ME

We cannot avoid contrasting the submission of God's will of Eli, Jonathan, and John the Baptist with the envy manifested by Saul when he learned that David would replace his sons as king. He personally placed David in danger by demanding a hundred foreskins of the Philistines as the dowry for his daughter, Michal, whom he offered to David for a wife. He hoped David would be killed. He twice attempted to nail David to the wall with his spear. He killed the priests at Nob who aided David, and repeatedly chased him through the wilderness seeking his life. God had said "no" to Saul, but Saul took out his frustration on the man to whom God had said "yes."

We might also contrast the response of King Ahab. The Lord had delivered the Syrian King Benhadad into the hands of Ahab for destruction. Ahab had released him, let him go, and had made a covenant with him through a prophet. The Lord announced that because he had released Benhadad, his life would be required in exchange for Benhadad's life, and his people for Benhadad's people. When God said "no" to Ahab, Ahab went to his house "resentful and sullen" (1 Kings 20:43).

We have all been tempted to be envious when our personal ambitions have been thwarted. We have all observed the person who could find no good in the job done by the one who got the position he wanted. He may promptly resign his previous position, or his resentment can take the form of sulking and declining to do anything, or of doing what he does only with bad will. He may attack the character of the person who displaced him; he may oppose every proposal made or every nominee to the organization.

99

Someone once commented (whether justly or not, I have no way of knowing) that opposition over a major project—opposition so strong that it brought division to the church—would never have occurred if certain individuals had not been by-passed.

There are many services in the Lord's vineyard. Some carry more prominence than others. All cannot be apostles; all apostles cannot be among the chosen three; and all three cannot be Peter. The question, "Who is to be the greatest in the kingdom of heaven?" (Matt. 18:1) has plagued every generation of the church from its very beginning. When the Lord says that you are not worthy of the task for which you have nominated yourself, the best thing for you to do is say with Eli, "It is the Lord; let him do what seems good to him" (1 Sam. 3:18), and then find the service you *can* render.

14

The Ministry of Study

A short time ago I picked up a publicity folder from a school which described the various community services in which its students participated. Some were engaged in the ministry of singing, of teaching, of visitation, and others were preaching. Some were in a ministry to the sick and some to the poor, some ministered in the inner city and some to the suburbs; but the caption which caught my eye was one over a student at work at his desk. It read "The Ministry of Study."

Many people seem to feel that study is one of the optional activities of preaching to be engaged in by a few individuals strange enough to enjoy it. Or, if not optional, at the best it is a necessary evil to which only a minimal amount of time should be devoted. Some vigorously resist learning anything new and others seem to feel that depth of study endangers the soul. What a striking idea the brochure had: "The Ministry of Study"!

While some men still take pride in their lack of training, long ago the rabbis said that no one is as poor as is the ignoramus.[1] They also said that the Torah is not a crown with which to adorn one's self nor is it a spade with which to dig.[2] That is to say, that study is to be thought of neither as a means of self-aggrandizement nor as a mere way to gain a livelihood. I would like to challenge you to think of your study as a ministry rendered in service to God.

THE BATTLE FOR THE MINDS OF MEN

Our world is gripped as never before in a gigantic struggle for control of the minds of men. In this struggle, what will eventually win out? What sort of world will tomorrow's world be?

Our congregations are growing; but we are faced with a rapidly increasing world population which is expanding much more rapidly, percentage-wise, than is Christianity. Unless the trend is reversed and the advance of Christianity is stepped up, the world of tomorrow will not be a Christian world. Although in America (as of 1981) 58.7 percent of the people claim church me..nbership, on any particular week there are actually fewer and fewer people sitting on the pews of the churches while more and more are in bed, on the golf links, at the races, or at the beaches.

Coupled with the increase in world population, there is also a rapidly rising educational level in the world public and especially of the American public. In the small Texas town in which I grew up, I do not recall there being any person in town with a Ph.D. degree. Only a decided minority had been to college. Out of my graduating class of thirty-five, perhaps six to ten went to college. The small college I attended had at that time only three or four Ph.D.'s on its entire staff, and they were regarded with special respect for their attainments. In the same school today most departments would have more men than that with the Ph.D. degree. And so it is in all our society; the educational trend is upward with no signs of leveling off. In the pioneer days, any man could come out of the cornfield and start preaching. Great sacrifices were made and great service was rendered by these men, but the day has passed in America when any sizable number of people will listen to the cornfield preacher.

Paul said, we struggle "to take every thought captive to obey Christ" (2 Cor. 10:5). We in the church cannot afford to write off as a total loss the educated segment of our population. Yet, a short

102

time back I heard a man say of preaching, "All you need to preach are a few Scriptures and the gift of gab." I doubt we are going to make much progress in this ideological war in which we are involved if God's servants as their training have only "a few Scriptures and the gift of gab." In contrast to this shortsighted attitude Bacon said:

> Let no man out of a weak conceit of sobriety, or an ill-applied moderation, think or maintain that a man can search too far or be too well studied in the book of God's Word, or in the book of God's works; divinity or philosophy; but rather let men endeavor an endless progress of proficiency in both.[3]

YOUR PLACE, AS A STUDENT, IN THE WAR

If you are now students, there will probably be no other time in your life when you will have equal time and opportunity to read the books and get the equipment that one needs to be an effective proclaimer of the Word of God. It is easy to say that time will be more available when you graduate, but that is a delusion. I regularly encounter the student who is so involved in part-time employment, who is so excited about getting to the mission field, that he has no time to study. He reminds me of a story one of my friends tells of a man cutting weeds with a dull hoe who insisted that he had too many weeds to cut to be able to take time out to sharpen his hoe. Though they affirm personal willingness to go where the Lord would have them go, to make whatever sacrifices may be needed, and to face untold dangers if they arise, for many men the discipline of the study desk is just not what they have in mind.

There are many students of whose ideals and dreams I approve, but I cannot get very excited about their achieving them because of the careless school work they are doing now. Elton Trueblood has said that we may well question the genuineness of the Christian experience of the student who says he is a Christian but who will not get his work in on time. The man who cannot take time to prepare himself is dooming himself to a life of frustration. He becomes like a carpenter trying to cut a 2 x 4 with a coping saw or trying to drive a spike with a tack hammer.

The rabbis said that for the duty of leaving the corners of fields unharvested, for gleanings, and for loving deeds there are no prescribed limits of the Law.[4] I would add to that list that "for study" there is no limit. My younger son at an earlier stage in his schooling had somewhat the attitude that study is confined to the three problems the teacher had assigned for the next day. The library might be full of books that he has not read, but there was no possibility of his doing more than the three problems. Students will say, "I have your lecture notes" as though that is all they needed. Is education merely what you can get as the lecture goes by? One has said, "The physical resource for Christian spirituality most open to all seminaries is the library."[5] And again, "However, a richly endowed library will be of little use unless there is an awareness on the part of students of how the collection should be used."[6]

One of the rabbis said, "A man can only obtain knowledge by sacrifice."[7] You must apply the seat of your pants to a chair for long periods of time. Two to three hours should be spent out of class in preparation for each hour spent in class. This means that if you are taking twelve hours, then twenty-four to thirty-six hours should be spent in study. That makes a total of forty-eight hours a week minimum. This time often should be even greater when you are studying at the graduate level. If outside demands on your time prohibit that much time, then you must take a reduced load and extend the time you are in school. There is a great deal of difference in getting a degree and in getting an education. Rather than education being "three problems" or complying with minimum course requirements, it is absorbing all you can absorb and then still thirsting for more. The record you make in school is extremely important. All future academic admissions, as far as you are concerned, will be determined by it. All scholarship applications will be decided by it. Wise future employers will look it over before they hire you: and when you ask one of your teachers for a recommendation (which you will want to do), he will first think of your school fidelity. This is the period in which lifelong habits are formed. "He that is faithful in a very little is faithful also in much" (Luke 16:10).

As H. R. Niebuhr said:

> A theological education which does not lead young men and women to embark on a continuous, ever-incomplete but ever-sustained effort to study and to understand the meaning of their work and of the situations in which they labor is neither theological nor education.[8]

Long ago a wise man said, "What thy hand finds to do, do it with thy might" (Eccl. 9:10). Think of your study program as a "ministry of study" rendered to God.

A LIFELONG PROGRAM OF SELF-IMPROVEMENT

The preacher needs to plan for a life which involves a ministry of study. Yet one of the preachers in our town openly states that he does not like to study, and all about him would say that his preaching reflects it. There is first the weekly chore of preparation of two or more sermons. Whereas some good speakers have only one or two good speeches and change their audiences regularly, the preacher (without benefit of the ghost writer) must either come up with challenging lessons week after week or move on to a new place. Yet all of our bookstore managers say that their biggest market among preachers is not for solid study tools but for sermon outline books. We will not win the war for the minds of men with borrowed sermon outlines.

Someone has compared studying and preaching to putting water into a tank. At studying you fill the tank with a one inch pipe; when speaking you are letting it out with a ten inch pipe. I have always felt the incoming pipe in my case was about a one-fourth inch one. A well-prepared sermon may take as much as twenty hours spent in its preparation. When you are young and vivacious the magnetism of personality gets you a hearing; but when you get into the "5 B" class (baldness, bifocals, bridgework, bay window, and bunions), what will you offer?

Many preachers are excited about investments. There are some who think that life insurance is the thing you should put your money in. Others think it should be real estate. Still others are adept at playing the stock market. The best investment you can make is your investment in yourself.

Never mind how brilliant he is, a man's judgment is only as good as his information. R. Jose said: "Fit yourself for the study of the Law, for the knowledge of it is not yours by inheritance."[9] R. Eleazar ben Azariah said: "If there is no study of the Law there is no fitting behaviour."[10] As a preacher you need time in your schedule, not directly related to sermon preparation, when you are not available for the telephone—a time when your wife and children are not running in and out carrying on a conversation—a time in which you will sharpen up your Greek and Hebrew. Have you ever thought of the presumption there is in passing yourself off as an interpreter of a book that you cannot read? You need a time to sharpen up the areas of biblical knowledge in which you have competency. The preacher should primarily be an expert in Scripture—yet how often this fails to be true! You need a time to widen your knowledge into areas where you perhaps are not yet competent: church history, the world of the Bible, social problems, and philosophy. It is much easier to spend your time in "administrivia," in counseling, in gabbing, and in coffee drinking than in honest labor—"the ministry of study."

"Let us press on to know the Lord" (Hos. 6:3). "He that ministers, let him give himself to his ministry" (Rom. 12:7).

NOTES

[1] T. B. Ned. 62a.

[2] M. Ned. 40:1.

[3] Francis Bacon, *Advancement of Learning*, First Book, 1, 3.

[4] T. J. Peah 1 No. 1.

[5] C. Feilding, *Education for the Ministry* (Dayton: American Assoc. Theol. Schools, 1966), pp. 171, 94.

[6] Ibid., p. 94.

[7] T. B. Berakoth 60:3.

[8] H. R. Niebuhr, *The Purpose of the Church and Its Ministry* (New York: Harper & Brothers, 1956), p. 134.

[9] M. Aboth 2:12.

[10] M. Aboth 3:18.

15

Tell Us the Dream

When Nebuchadnezzar called in his wise men to interpret his dream, they immediately said, "Tell us the dream, and we will show its interpretation" (Dan. 2:7). After the king could not relate the dream, they replied that no man on earth could meet the king's demand and that no king had ever made such an unreasonable demand as to require that his wise men give him the interpretation of a dream when he, himself, did not know what the dream was (Dan. 2:10).

This episode may suggest to us one of the major factors needed in order to accomplish our goals—both in our projects within the congregations and in our mission projects. Since we have not stated adequately to ourselves what our dream is, we do not know what steps to take to accomplish it; and though we are busy, we are disappointed at the outcome. Out of the dream comes the interpretation and not the other way around.

Accrediting agencies for schools place great stress upon an adequate statement of purpose. Many schools experience the need of reworking their statement of purpose several times until the board, administration, and faculty have come to a meeting of minds concerning what they are trying to do and can clearly state to others this purpose. It is obvious that there is no merit in a statement of purpose in and of itself. Why then all this stress on it? The answer is simple. The people who are unclear on what their dreams are or who can only state them in vague generalities will also be vague on how to proceed from where they are to where they want to be. They are at a loss when it comes to evaluating their progress or regression. If a group is concerned, they may even be working at cross purposes with each other, and they may be engaged in activity that will make the ultimate realization of their dream impossible. Few things are more important than a definition of aims.

I am not convinced that the kingdom of heaven is really advanced by "activity in the congregation" in and for itself. The teacher who spends three-fourths of her time on handwork and one-fourth on the lesson has not clarified in her mind what she is trying to accomplish. The youth leader whose major drive is "keeping the young people busy" needs to take another look at his dream. The preacher who brags that everybody is busy needs to be clear as to what is really being accomplished. The devil is also quite busy.

All Christians today are grateful for the great enthusiasm for mission work that has been built up in the congregations and we wish there were even greater enthusiasm. But, in some cases we have spent much both in time and money and seem to have accomplished little. One factor is that the congregation had one dream and the man they selected to help accomplish it had another. Another factor is that neither of them was adequately clear on what their dream was. "Going to the mission field" and "converting the world" are not clear statements. It is easy for a congregation to be on fire to send and for a person to be on fire to go while neither of them has any clear picture of the concrete thing they intend to accomplish. Once in the field, the man with confused aims experiences frustration, blindly plunges here and there, and accomplishes little. A man may be of unreproachable Christian character and be of ultimate dedication and still be hazy on what really is his dream. Is the growth of the kingdom a thing that is bound to take place if people have good intentions? Or is that growth the result of intelligent procedure—which depends upon God's blessings—but which has learned from the mistakes of the past and carefully engages in self-evaluation?

There are certain types of dreams that are almost certain to end in frustration. When young I went to the mission field with the dream of reaching the masses through the "big splash" approach. Newspaper advertising was to afford the needed contacts. I learned the hard way that you seldom attract stable people by the "big splash." You get the "shoppers" upon whom you cannot depend and who will shop elsewhere in a little while. If your dream is to win "faithful men who will teach others also" (2 Tim. 2:2), this approach will not accomplish it. Is not the same verdict to be rendered on other types of programs—of whatever nature—from which the major response can be expected from the unstable and from the malcontents?

Saving the lives of men in various types of charitable activity is a very worthwhile undertaking (Matt. 25). Raising their standard of living is also admirable. The problem arises when we invariably think that by the same process we will win souls. Instead of winning souls, it may well be a block to winning souls. We seriously need to ask whether our dream is saving lives, improving the economic level, or saving souls. Jesus discovered that he could feed five thousand men and they would receive it, but when he talked about the Bread of Life, he lost them all (John 6). In the present day the charity approach seems first to attract those seeking a "free ride" and, having attracted them, it locks and bars the door against attracting men of self-respect who could become "faithful men to teach others." In some fields it does not take much charity to bring about this frustration where every person in attendance is receiving material benefit and the work cannot command the respect of anyone. Define your dreams and you will better know what to do next.

Educating people is a very worthwhile activity. The planting and nurture of the Gospel is a continuous process of education. But, we need some clear thinking about whether our dream is raising the educational level of a selected number of people or whether our primary drive is to convert them and equip them for heaven. These two aims may prove mutually exclusive of each other. Recently a capable young man asked me to help him to go to America for educational purposes. He frankly said, "The political situation here has become intolerable for us." I do not care to dispute his assertion. Rescuing him from an intolerable situation would be a charitable act, but I doubt it would advance the kingdom of God one iota. On the contrary, it would attract to the church other young men whose real motive (though not at first revealed) would be to be likewise rescued, and it would repel good and honest hearts.

When you are thinking of sending a man to the mission field, it would be worth your while first to find out clearly what is your own dream and second to find out how clear is his dream. It will avoid frustration for both of you.

DREAMS WE OUGHT TO BE DREAMING

We ought to be dreaming of learning the language of the people with whom we are working. Every time I speak through an interpreter and every time I attend a service where an interpreter is used, I ask myself, "If I were in the pew, would I listen to such teaching and would I be greatly influenced by it?" The answer is invariably the same: "I would not." The stable people of various societies we are trying to reach are not different. Our government trains its diplomats in the language of the area where they will work. The church needs to do the same. As long as we depend on interpreters we can expect to be "taken in" on financial transactions and can expect to reap a minimal harvest for the labor expended.

We need a dream of becoming involved in the lives of the people who are lost in ways that will remold their lives without dangling any material attraction before them. The impersonal approach is easier and perhaps more attractive for the moment. The material appeal affords a basis for glowing reports, but when the air has cleared, there is little left behind.

We need a dream of growth in the kingdom that will not demand that a man either paint glowing progress reports or feel that his support may be in jeopardy. In the mission field solid growth is painfully slow and it is quite needful that after a few months or years we still have a few of those we have baptized. All is not glowing. The broomweed grows in a few months, but it takes an oak longer.

We need a dream which has an abundance of Christian charity, but which is not willing to compromise the truth of God. Why should we be willing to find "an indigenous Restoration Movement" in the mission field that we would not at all fellowship if both we and they were back home? Why should we expect the providence of God to overrule for good in the mission field our tolerance for that which is untruthful and unchristian?

Some brethren are giving out the figures that our average missionary spends from two to two and one-half years in the field and then comes home to stay. Never mind explaining what the causes are. Without intending to cast aspersions on the contribution of any, we need dreams of whole lives of service that find meaning rather than the semi-persecution complex of self-sacrifice in the work they are doing. We need dreams that do not find the present assignment merely a temporary arrangement until one can do the work to which he really wishes to give himself.

We need dreams of stable programs that will allow a man to work in peace to the best of his ability. I know of works where the relationship between the supporting congregation and the workers is pathetically poor. The workers seem continuously in fear that their supporting congregations will cut them off. A man cannot do a creditable work under these conditions. If you do not have the confidence in your workers that will enable you to give them security, bring them home and put the Lord's money to a better use. If you do have confidence, assure your man of it that he may give himself to the task to which you have committed him.

Define your aims clearly. Tell us your dream and we will tell you the interpretation (outcome).